MONTREUX
TRAVEL GUIDE 2024,
SWITZERLAND

Embark on an Alpine Adventure through Culture, Cuisine, and Hidden Gems in Montreux 2024 .

Helsi Robson

MONTREUX TRAVEL GUIDE 2024

Copyright © (Helsi Robson), (2024).

All rights reserved. No part of this publication may be reproduced, distributed, or transmitted in any form or by any means, including photocopying, recording, or other electronic or mechanical methods, without the prior written permission of the publisher, except in the case of brief quotations embodied in critical reviews and certain other noncommercial uses permitted by copyright law.

MONTREUX TRAVEL GUIDE 2024

TABLE OF CONTENT

INTRODUCTION..4
    Overview of Montreux 2024................................5
    What Makes Montreux a Thrill-Seeker's Paradise?..8
PLANNING YOUR TRIP..11
    Visa Requirements and Travel Documents.............11
    Best Time to Visit Montreux................................... 16
    Weather and Packing Tips..20
    Currency and Money Matters.................................. 25
    Language and Local Etiquette................................. 29
ACCOMMODATION OPTIONS..32
    Luxury Hotels with Alpine Views.............................. 32
    Cozy Boutique Inns and Bed & Breakfasts............. 36
    Budget-Friendly Hostels for Backpackers...............42
    Unique Stays(Chalets and Airbnb Experiences).....45
CRAFTING THE PERFECT ITINERARY.....................48
    Day 1: Lakeside Promenada Exploration............... 48
    Day 2: Outdoor Adventures in the Swiss Alps........ 50
    Day 3: Culinary Delights in Montreux...................... 53
    Day 4: Off-the-Beaten-Path Discoveries.................55
    Day 5: Relaxation and Spa Day...............................59
OUTDOOR ACTIVITIES...61
    Hiking Trails with Breathtaking Views..................... 61
    Water Sports on Lake Geneva................................63
    Skiing and Snowboarding in the Nearby.................67
    Paragliding Adventures Over Montreux...................70
ADRENALINE-PUMPING EXPERIENCES...................75

Bungee Jumping from the Verzasca Dam............. 75
Skydiving with Panoramic Alpine Vistas................ 78
Mountain Biking Trails for Thrill-Seekers................ 81
Rock Climbing in the Swiss Riviera....................... 85

NIGHTLIFE AND ENTERTAINMENT......................... 89
Trendy Bars and Nightclubs in Montreux...............89
Jazz and Music Festivals in the Region.................93
Casino Montreux(Gaming and Glamour)...............97

LOCAL CUISINE..100
Swiss Fondue(A Culinary Must-Try)................... 100
Traditional Alpine Dishes..................................... 103
Gourmet Dining Overlooking Lake Geneva.......... 106
Best Cafés for Swiss Chocolate and Pastries....... 111

POPULAR MUSEUMS...115
Montreux Jazz Heritage....................................... 115
Chillon Castle... 118
Swiss Museum of Games.................................... 121
Charlie Chaplin's World in Vevey.........................123

DAY TRIPS...126
Excursion to Zermatt and the Matterhorn............ 126
Geneva.. 128
Lavaux Vineyards.. 131
Rochers-de-Naye...134

PRACTICAL TIPS FOR THRILL-SEEKERS............. 137
Emergency Contacts and Medical Facilities......... 137
Transportation Options in Montreux.....................140
Safety Precautions for Outdoor Adventures......... 143
CONCLUSION... 147

INTRODUCTION

Welcome to the Montreux Travel Guide 2024, Switzerland your gateway to an Alpine paradise where every moment is a masterpiece. In the pages that follow, we invite you to explore the captivating landscapes, rich culture, and hidden treasures that define this lakeside gem. This is not just a guide; it's an immersive experience that transcends the ordinary and invites you to embrace the extraordinary.

As you turn the pages of this guide, you'll notice a deliberate choice: no maps, no images. Why, you may ask? Because we believe in the power of words to paint vivid landscapes and ignite the imagination. We want you to embark on this journey with a blank canvas, allowing the descriptions to come to life in your mind's eye. It's an invitation to see Montreux through your own unique perspective, to feel the rhythm of the lakeside promenade, to taste the richness of Swiss fondue, and to envision the majesty of the Swiss Alps.

In a world inundated with visuals, we challenge you to rediscover the joy of exploration through the art of storytelling. The absence of maps is an intentional choice – an encouragement to get lost in the charm of Montreux, to stumble upon hidden gems, and to navigate the cityscape with a sense of wonder.

So, as you embark on this literary journey, let the words be your guide. Immerse yourself in the enchanting tales of Montreux, and let your imagination carve out the paths and vistas that will make your adventure uniquely yours.

Welcome to Montreux a place where beauty lies not just in what you see, but in how you see it. Let the exploration begin.

Overview of Montreux 2024

Montreux, a lovely lakeside town nestled among the stunning backdrop of the Swiss Riviera, has captured travellers for generations with its compelling combination of natural beauty, cultural attractions, and active atmosphere. Montreux provides a lovely getaway from the everyday, perched on the banks of Lake Geneva with the magnificent Alps as a background, beckoning you to discover its rich history, immerse yourself in its dynamic cultural scene, and revel in the joys of its famous cuisine.

An Entrance to Swiss Charm: Montreux's attractiveness stems from its seamless blend of historic Swiss charm and cosmopolitan flare. Its charming lanes dotted with exquisite Belle Époque hotels and vivacious cafés radiate a sophisticated elegance, while the wall-preserved mediaeval castle, Château de Chillon, bears witness to its rich past.

A Musician's Paradise: Montreux has long been a music lover's sanctuary, hosting the world-famous Montreux Jazz Festival, an annual celebration of jazz music that draws renowned musicians from all over the world. Beyond jazz, the town's musical tradition includes a thriving classical music culture and a number of small performance spaces.

A Delectable Delight: Montreux's culinary scene is a symphony of flavours, appealing to all palates. The town's gastronomic environment is as varied as its attractions, ranging from Michelin-starred restaurants serving superb gourmet dishes to cosy cafés providing traditional Swiss food.

An Outdoor Adventurer's Paradise: Montreux, surrounded by the magnificent surroundings of the Swiss Riviera, provides a wealth of outdoor excursions for nature lovers. Hike or cycle along gorgeous pathways through vineyards and woodlands, cool off in Lake Geneva or fly over the Alps in a spectacular paragliding trip.

A Cultural Paradise: Montreux is a cultural haven, with a plethora of museums, art galleries, and theatres. Discover Freddie Mercury's intriguing world at the Queen Studio Experience, dig into the region's history at the Musée du Vieux-Montreux, or experience a thrilling concert at the Stravinski Auditorium.

A Four-Season Destination: Montreux is a year-round resort with a distinct appeal in each season. Spring brings blossoming flowers to the town, summer brings outdoor dining and lakeside activities, fall colours the environment, and winter turns the town into a winter wonderland.

Whether you're looking for cultural immersion, outdoor activities, or just a calm retreat, Montreux welcomes you with open arms, eager to reveal its enthralling combination of natural beauty, cultural riches, and timeless elegance.

What Makes Montreux a Thrill-Seeker's Paradise?

Montreux, set among the gorgeous surroundings of the Swiss Riviera, is a refuge for thrill-seekers looking for a thrilling mix of adventure, adrenaline-pumping activities, and spectacular natural beauty.

Aquatic Activities:

Lake Geneva: Plunge into Lake Geneva's crystal-clear waters, where a range of water sports await. Set off on an exciting sailing adventure, put your balance to the test on a stand-up paddleboard, or experience the adrenaline of kitesurfing, which uses the strength of the wind to push you over the lake's surface.

Aerial Adventure:

Paragliding: Soar high over the Swiss Riviera's stunning scenery, dangling underneath a colourful paraglider. As you soar through the air, take in stunning aerial views of the city, Lake Geneva, and the beautiful Alps.

Hang Gliding: Experience pure excitement of hang gliding by throwing oneself from a mountainside and soaring gently across the valleys, taking in panoramic views of the surrounding area.

Terrestrial Excitement:

Hike: Lace up your hiking boots and go off on exhilarating hikes along the region's scenic routes. Immerse yourself in the serene splendour of the Swiss countryside by exploring the vineyards and woods that coat the slopes around Montreux.

Mountain Biking: Adrenaline-pumping mountain bike tracks meander across the mountains, providing spectacular vistas and exciting descents. Feel the surge of excitement as you traverse the difficult terrain while surrounded by the breathtaking landscape of the Alps.

City Adventures:

Canyoning: Descend waterfalls, abseil down steep cliffs, and navigate through secret gorges on an amazing canyoning trip. As you tackle the hurdles of this adrenaline-fueled exercise, feel the rush of pushing your limitations.

Rafting on Whitewater: A whitewater rafting excursion through the rapids of neighbouring rivers will put your abilities and fortitude to the best. Feel the thrill of adrenaline as you navigate the rushing currents while surrounded by the natural splendour of the Swiss nature.

Montreux combines natural beauty, cultural attractions, and exhilarating activities, making it a great location for adrenaline seekers looking for an exceptional experience. Montreux delivers a thrilling vacation that will leave you breathless and needing more, whether you're flying through the sky, negotiating tough paths, or diving into the depths of Lake Geneva.

PLANNING YOUR TRIP

Visa Requirements and Travel Documents

Montreux, Switzerland Visa Requirements and Travel Documents

A journey to Montreux, situated among the stunning landscape of the Swiss Riviera, requires careful consideration of visa requirements and travel papers. Understanding the appropriate papers enables a smooth and flawless visit, whether you're a thrill-seeker looking for adrenaline-pumping thrills or a cultural aficionado attracted to its rich legacy.

Exemptions from Citizenship and Visas

The visa requirements for Montreux vary according to your country. Citizens of most nations, including the United States, Canada, Australia, New Zealand, and the majority of European Union countries, may visit Switzerland without a visa for stays of up to 90 days. There are certain exceptions, therefore it's essential to check your visa status with the Swiss embassy or consulate in your home country before leaving.

Must-Have Travel Documents for Visa-Free Travellers

If you are a citizen of a visa-exempt nation, you must have the following papers with you while enter in Switzerland:

1. Valid Passport: Make sure you have at least two blank pages in your passport to accept visa stamps or entry/exit stamps.

2. Proof of Onward or Return Travel: Provide a verified return ticket or further travel schedule to demonstrate your purpose to leave Switzerland.

3. Proof of Adequate Financial Means: Persuade the immigration officials that you have enough money to maintain yourself throughout your stay in Switzerland. This may be shown by bank statements, credit card statements, or traveler's checks.

4. Travel Insurance: Protect your health and safety by purchasing comprehensive travel insurance that includes medical bills, repatriation, and emergency help.

5. Accommodation Details: Provide proof of your lodging arrangements, such as hotel bookings or Airbnb confirmations.

Additional Materials: You may be requested to supply additional papers, such as a letter of invitation from a Swiss resident or firm, evidence of enrollment in a Swiss educational institution, or a vaccination certificate for certain illnesses, depending on your individual circumstances.

How to Apply for a Visa for Non-Exempt Nationals

If you are a citizen of a nation that needs a visa to visit Switzerland, you must apply for the visa well in advance of your trip. Visa requirements differ based on your nationality and the reason of your visit. However, you will often be required to produce the following documents:

1. Full Visa Application Form: Download and carefully fill out the Swiss visa application form, making sure that all areas are correctly filled out.

2. Two Passport-Size Photos: Submit two current passport-sized pictures that fulfil the Swiss visa office's particular standards.

Valid Passport: Present your valid passport, which should have at least two blank pages for visa stamps or entry/exit stamps.

4. Proof of Onward or Return Travel: To indicate your plan to leave Switzerland, provide a confirmed return ticket or further travel schedule.

5. Proof of Adequate Financial Means: Present bank statements, credit cards, or traveler's checks that show you have sufficient funds for your stay in Switzerland to demonstrate financial stability.

6. Travel Insurance: Obtain comprehensive travel insurance that covers medical costs, repatriation, and emergency help while in Switzerland.

7. Accommodation Details: Provide proof of your lodging arrangements, such as hotel bookings or Airbnb confirmations.

8. Additional Materials: Depending on your specific situation, you may be required to present additional papers such as a letter of invitation from a Swiss resident or firm, evidence of participation in a Swiss educational institution, or a vaccination certificate for certain illnesses.

Interview and Visa Processing

You may be needed to attend a visa interview at the Swiss embassy or consulate in your country in certain situations. Prepare to answer questions about your travel plans, the purpose of your visit, and any other information during the interview.

The processing period for a Swiss visa application varies based on your nationality and the Swiss visa office's workload. To prevent any last-minute hassles, apply well in advance of your scheduled vacation.

How to Keep Your Visa and Travel Documents

Once you've gotten a Swiss visa, make sure you have it with you when you cross the border into Switzerland. Maintain the security and accessibility of your visa and other travel papers during your stay in the nation.

Looking for Advice and Updates

Always visit the official website of the Swiss embassy or consulate in your country for the most current and up-to-date information on visa requirements and travel papers for Montreux,

Switzerland. Their assistance will guarantee a seamless and compliant admission into Montreux's enchanting town.

Best Time to Visit Montreux

Montreux, set among the stunning beauty of the Swiss Riviera, enchants visitors all year, with each season bringing its own special fascination. Montreux welcomes you with open arms, whether you seek outdoor experiences, cultural immersion, or just a calm vacation.

Summer (June-September)

Summer is peak season in Montreux, with warm, sunny weather suitable for visiting its lakeside promenada, eating outside, and engaging in outdoor activities. During this season, the average temperature varies from 18°C to 25°C (64°F to 77°F).

Summer highlights in Montreux include:

1. The Montreux Jazz Festival, a world-famous jazz music event held in July that attracts renowned musicians from throughout the world.

2. Open-air concerts and performances at different locations throughout town.

3. A variety of festivals and events, including the Fête des Vignerons, a classic wine festival held every 25 years.

Fall (September to November)

Autumn paints Montreux in a colourful palette, with the neighbouring vineyards and woods providing a magnificent background. With typical temperatures ranging from 10°C to 15°C (50°F to 59°F), the weather is still nice, but colder than in the summer.

Autumn highlights in Montreux include:

1. A train ride on the Golden Pass Express that provides spectacular views of the Swiss Alps and surrounding region.

2. Hikes through vineyards and woodlands that showcase the changing leaf colours.

3. Culinary treats such as raclette, a typical Swiss meal of melted cheese fondue accompanied with potatoes and pickled gherkins.

Winter (December-February)

Montreux is transformed into a stunning winter wonderland in the winter, with the town decked up in festive lights and decorations. During this season, the average temperature ranged from -2°C to 5°C (28°F to 41°F).

Winter highlights in Montreux include:

1. The Montreux Christmas Market, a beautiful market packed with traditional Swiss Christmas decorations, handicrafts, and gastronomic delights.

2. Ice skating on the Place du Casino rink, a great winter pastime in the middle of the town's festive ambiance.

3. Skiing and snowboarding aficionados may visit neighbouring destinations such as Villars-sur-Ollon and Les Diablerets.

Spring (March-May)

Montreux comes alive with flowering flowers in the spring, transforming the town into a dazzling display of colours. Temperatures rise steadily, with averages ranging from 8°C to 18°C (46°F to 64°F).

Spring highlights in Montreux include:

1. Narcissus hikes, which are guided excursions through fields of narcissus flowers that bloom in the area at this time of year.

2. The Montreux Comedy Festival, a worldwide comedy event involving stand-up comedians, improv troupes, and sketch comedy shows.

3. The open-air season begins, with concerts and shows returning to different places across town.

Finally, the optimum time to visit Montreux is determined by your own choices and interests. Summer is perfect if you like nice weather and plenty of outdoor activities. Fall is a wonderful time to visit if you want a more calm ambiance and spectacular fall scenery. Winter beckons for a joyful winter holiday or winter sports experiences. If you're attracted to the flowering beauty of spring and cultural activities, spring has its own distinct appeal.

Montreux delivers an amazing experience in every season, immersing you in its rich history, thriving cultural scene, and spectacular natural beauty.

Weather and Packing Tips

Montreux, located on the banks of Lake Geneva in the heart of the lovely Swiss Riviera, has a moderate climate with noticeable seasonal fluctuations. While the weather is typically beautiful all year, packing appropriately will guarantee you're well-prepared for any weather conditions you may experience.

Summer (June-September)

Summer is the prime season in Montreux, with warm, sunny weather ideal for enjoying the lakeside promenade, alfresco restaurants, and outdoor sports. Temperatures vary from 18°C to 25°C (64°F to 77°F) on average.

Summer Packing Hints:

1. Bring light, airy clothing Choose cotton, linen, or other lightweight textiles to remain cool and comfortable in hot weather.

2. Pack a swimsuit and a cover-up You'll want to be prepared for a refreshing dip or a leisurely swim with Lake Geneva just outside your door.

3. Bring a hat and sunglasses: Protect yourself from the sun's rays by wearing a fashionable hat and sunglasses.

4. Bring comfortable shoes You'll most likely be walking a lot, so bring comfortable shoes that will support your feet during your activities.

Fall (September to November)

Autumn paints Montreux in a vivid pallet of colours, with the neighbouring vineyards and woods providing a magnificent background. With typical temperatures ranging from 10°C to 15°C (50°F to 59°F), the weather stays nice, but colder than in the summer.

Autumn Packing Hints

1. Layer your clothes: Pack layers of clothes that you can readily alter to the changing situations as the temperatures shift between day and night.

2. A light jacket or jumper is recommended: On chilly nights or during unexpected rains, a simple jacket or jumper will keep you warm.

3. Bring comfortable walking shoes: Bring comfortable shoes to explore the town and its surroundings.

4. Please bring an umbrella: Autumn rains are usual, so bring an umbrella to remain dry in case of an unexpected deluge.

Winter (December-February)

Montreux is transformed into a stunning winter wonderland in the winter, with the town decked up in festive lights and decorations. During this season, the average temperature ranged from -2°C to 5°C (28°F to 41°F).

Winter Packing Hints:

1. Pack warm, insulated clothing: To remain comfortable in the harsh winter weather, pack thick coats, sweaters, hats, gloves, and scarves.

2. Think about waterproof boots: Snow may fall, so bring waterproof boots to keep your feet dry and toasty.

3. Be sure to include warm pants: Thermal pants will provide an additional layer of insulation against the cold.

4. Bring a hat and earmuffs: A warm hat and earmuffs will protect your head and ears from the winter cold.

Spring (March-May)

Montreux comes alive with flowering flowers in the spring, transforming the town into a dazzling display of colours. Temperatures rise steadily, with averages ranging from 8°C to 18°C (46°F to 64°F).

Spring Packing Hints

1. Pack many layers of clothing: Pack clothing that you can readily modify to the shifting temperatures as the weather changes from chilly to warm.

2. A raincoat or poncho should be included: Spring showers are possible, so bring a raincoat or poncho to remain dry if it rains unexpectedly.

3. Be sure to bring good walking shoes. Pack good walking shoes since spring is a terrific time to explore the town and its surroundings on foot.

4. Bring a reusable water bottle: A reusable water bottle will keep you hydrated during your activities.

General Montreux Packing Hints

1. Pack flexible apparel: Choose clothing that can be combined and matched to create numerous ensembles, which will save you packing room.

2. Roll your clothing rather than folding them: Rolling your garments might help you save room in your suitcase and avoid crashes.

3. Make use of packing cubes: Packing cubes might help you organise your stuff and locate what you need more easily.

4. Keep toiletries in travel-size containers: Toiletries should be packed in travel-sized containers no bigger than 100ml (3. 4 oz) to comply with airline requirements.

5. Consider luggage weight constraints: To avoid extra baggage costs, be aware of airline baggage weight restrictions.

6. Make space for souvenirs: Make sure you have enough room in your baggage for any mementos you may buy during your vacation.

Following these packing advice will ensure that you are well-prepared for all weather conditions that may arise during your vacation to Montreux, guaranteeing a pleasant and pleasurable stay in this charming Swiss town.

Currency and Money Matters

Montreux, like the rest of Switzerland, is governed by the Swiss franc (CHF). The Swiss franc is a strong and stable currency that is widely accepted at most Montreux enterprises.

Currency Exchange Locations

If you are coming from a nation where the currency is different, you will need to convert your money into Swiss francs. Montreux has various currency exchange bureau, including those near the train station, banks, and several hotels. You may also exchange currencies from ATMs, but be sure to verify the exchange rate and costs first.

ATMs

ATMs may be found around Montreux, and the majority of them accept foreign debit and credit cards. You may withdraw Swiss francs from ATMs, but be sure to verify the exchange rate and costs first.

Credit and debit cards are accepted.

In Montreux, major credit cards like Visa, Mastercard, and American Express are frequently accepted. Most products and services, including meals, lodging, and transportation, may be paid for using a credit card. However, some smaller shops may not take credit cards, so having extra cash on hand is usually a smart idea.

Tipping

Tipping is not required, but it is valued in Switzerland. If you are pleased with the service, you may leave a tip of 5-10% of the cost. You may tip in cash or charge it to your credit card.

Prices

Montreux prices are usually higher than in other regions of Europe. However, the quality of products and services has improved. Here are some samples of average Montreux prices:
Meal at a mid-priced restaurant:

CHF 30-50

Cup of coffee: CHF 4-6

Beer: CHF 6-8

Glass of wine: CHF 8-12

Taxi ride (short distance): CHF 15-20

Bus ticket: CHF 2-3

Train ticket (short distance): CHF 5-10

Hotel room (mid-range): CHF 150-200 per night

Additional Financial Advice

1. Maintain receipts for all purchases. This will make it easy to monitor your expenditure and get a refund if required.

2. Keep an eye on the currency rate. Because the exchange rate might vary on a daily basis, be sure to check the current rate before exchanging money or using your credit card.

3. Inform your bank that you will be away. This can assist you avoid having your card denied when travelling overseas.

4. Take care of your money. Carry just what you need, and be mindful of your surroundings while using your credit card.

By following these money-saving ideas, you may assure a financially rewarding and delightful vacation to Montreux.

Language and Local Etiquette

Montreux, a lovely lakeside town located among the stunning beauty of the Swiss Riviera, is a multilingual centre, with the most often spoken languages being French, German, and English. While English speakers are likely to be found in tourist areas and many restaurants, knowing some basic French phrases can improve your experience and display your appreciation for the local culture.

Essential French Phrases

Bonjour: Hello

Au revoir: Goodbye

Merci: Thank you

S'il vous plaît: Please

Excusez-moi: Excuse me

Je ne parle pas français: I don't speak French

Où sont les toilettes?: Where are the toilets?

Pouvez-vous m'aider?: Can you help me?

L'addition, s'il vous plaît: The bill, please

Local Etiquette

1. Greetings and farewells: A handshake is a typical greeting gesture. A simple "au revoir" or "à bientôt" (until soon) is suitable for farewells.

2. Dining Etiquette: In Montreux, table manners are typically respected. Keep your elbows off the table and your phone stowed away. When you're done eating, line up your knife and fork parallel on the plate, producing an inverted 'V' or 'X'.

3. Tipping is optional but much appreciated. A gratuity of 5-10% of the bill is usual for excellent service.

4. Public Transport: In Montreux, public transport is frequently utilised and efficient. The aged, handicapped, and pregnant women get priority seating.

5. Respecting Public Spaces: Be cautious of noise levels and avoid littering or causing damage to public property.

6. Dress Code: Montreux has a permissive dress code, however while visiting religious sites or attending formal occasions, it's best to dress modestly.

7. While English is frequently spoken, try to utilise French wherever feasible, particularly in non-tourist regions. This shows regard for the local language and culture.

8. Immerse yourself in the local culture by visiting museums, attending traditional festivals, and interacting with friendly inhabitants.

9. Gratitude: Express your appreciation for whatever help or compassion you receive. A simple "merci" may mean a lot.

Following these etiquette recommendations and learning some basic French words will help you navigate Montreux with confidence and respect for the local culture. Remember that putting forth a little effort may go a long way towards having a great and memorable travel experience.

ACCOMMODATION OPTIONS

Luxury Hotels with Alpine Views

1. Fairmont Le Montreux Palace: Dive in!
Enjoy the beauty and grandeur of Fairmont Le Montreux Palace, a luxury hotel on Lake Geneva's shoreline. This historic landmark, with its imposing façade and superb interiors, has been greeting visitors since 1901, hosting prominent personalities and celebrities throughout the years.

Step into a world of sophisticated luxury, with large apartments that provide stunning views of the lake and the beautiful Alps. Each room and suite is stylishly outfitted with luxurious furniture, marble baths, and cutting-edge facilities to provide a completely relaxing visit.

Indulge in culinary brilliance at one of the hotel's famous restaurants, each of which offers a distinct dining experience. The Michelin-starred La Montreux takes you to a realm of gourmet creativity, while the Montreux Jazz Café encourages you to savour wonderful food while enjoying live music performances.

Relax and relax at the Willow Stream Spa, a quiet oasis situated inside the hotel. Allow professional hands to personalis treatments to your specific requirements, leaving you feeling refreshed and revitalised.

2. Majestic Grand Hotel Suisse

At Grand Hotel Suisse Majestic, a Belle Époque jewel that emanates ageless elegance, embraces the charm of yesteryear. Since 1875, this magnificent lady has welcomed visitors from all over the world, providing a unique combination of historical atmosphere and contemporary conveniences.

Relax in elegantly decorated apartments, each intended to give maximum comfort and relaxation. Every area, from cosy single rooms to large suites, has gorgeous decor, marble baths, and contemporary conveniences.

Savour gastronomic pleasures in the hotel's famous restaurants, each of which offers a distinct culinary experience. The hotel's primary restaurant, Le Régence, features superb Swiss cuisine with a contemporary touch, while the La Palette restaurant provides a more relaxed dining experience with stunning lake views.

After a day of exploration, relax and revitalise in the hotel's spa centre. Massages, facials, and other rejuvenating treatment will leave you feeling revitalised and ready to start on new experiences.

3. The Royal Savoy Hotel and Spa
The Royal Savoy Hotel & Spa, an exquisite refuge only a short walk from Lake Geneva, welcomes you into a world of sophisticated luxury. This hotel provides a beautiful combination of heritage and modernity with its Belle Époque façade and contemporary interiors.

Relax in large rooms that combine comfort and elegance. Each room and suite has sumptuous furniture, marble baths, and cutting-edge facilities to provide a completely relaxing stay.

Explore the hotel's famous restaurants, each of which offers a distinct dining experience. In a bustling ambiance, the La Brasserie provides excellent Swiss and international food, while the Le Montreux Jazz Club encourages guests to savour gourmet cuisine while listening to live music performances.

Pamper yourself at the hotel's spa, a relaxing and rejuvenating haven. Massages and facials, as well as body wraps and hydrotherapy, are among the rejuvenating treatments available, leaving you feeling refreshed and revitalised.

4. Mirador Kempinski Montreux
Mirador Kempinski Montreux, a grandiose resort nestle on the Montreux mountaintop, is the height of luxury. With breathtaking views of Lake Geneva and the Alps, this hotel provides an amazing retreat from the everyday.

Immerse yourself in luxurious and comfortable lodgings. Each room and suite has sumptuous furniture, marble baths, and cutting-edge facilities to provide a completely relaxing stay.

Explore the hotel's famous restaurants, each of which offers a distinct dining experience. The Le Cap Horn restaurant serves delicious seafood with stunning lake views, while Les Délices d'Orient serves traditional Thai cuisine.

Experience peace in the hotel's spa, a sanctuary of calm hidden among spectacular vistas. Massages and facials, as well as body wraps and hydrotherapy, are among the regenerative treatments available, leaving you feeling refreshed and revitalised.

5. Hôtel des Trois Couronnes

Hôtel des Trois Couronnes, a Belle Époque treasure that has adorned the shores of Lake Geneva since 1856, transports you back in time. This ancient hotel, with its attractive façade and excellent decor, provides a combination of traditional Swiss hospitality and contemporary conveniences.

Relax in elegantly designed sites that honour the hotel's historic history. Each room and suite has antique antiques, marble baths, and contemporary facilities to make your stay absolutely unforgettable.

Enjoy gastronomic pleasures at one of the hotel's famous restaurants.

Cozy Boutique Inns and Bed & Breakfasts

Montreux, a picturesque lakeside town hidden among the stunning beauty of the Swiss Riviera, has a great assortment of cosy boutique inns and bed & breakfasts that provide a warm and friendly alternative to typical hotels. These tiny lodgings often inhabit old buildings, oozing a distinct character and charm that immerses visitors in the town's rich history.

1. La Maison du Vigneron
La Maison du Vigneron, located in the centre of Montreux's old town, provides a calm respite from the city's hustle and bustle. With exposed stone walls, wooden beams, and cosy fireplaces, this quaint bed & breakfast, built in a 17th-century vineyard keeper's home, oozes rustic elegance.

Each of the six beautifully furnished rooms offers a distinctive combination of classic charm and contemporary conveniences. Guests may relax in sumptuous mattresses, rest in cosy sitting spaces, and enjoy views of the neighbouring vineyards from select suites.

The pleasant and friendly ambiance of La Maison du Vigneron is emphasised by the attentive service of the hosts, who make visitors feel at ease. Begin your day with a delightful breakfast served in the attractive dining room or courtyard, which includes fresh local food and handcrafted specialties.

2. Pension Rosier

Pension Rosier, located only a short distance from the beaches of Lake Geneva, provides a beautiful combination of Swiss warmth and contemporary conveniences. This family-run bed and breakfast is set in a typical chalet-style property and has a welcoming environment.

Each of the eight attractively appointed rooms has comfy mattresses, private bathrooms, and lovely balconies with views of the lake or garden. Guests may unwind in the cosy living room with a fireplace, swim in the outdoor pool, or rest on the sun terrace with views of the lake and the Alps.

Pension Rosier's welcoming staff are dedicated to providing visitors with an unforgettable stay. They give personalised suggestions for seeing the region's sights, help with transportation and activities, and provide a great breakfast every day that includes fresh local vegetables and handmade delights.

3. Le Petit Verger

Le Petit Verger, perched on a hillside above Montreux, provides a peaceful haven among lush nature. With exposed stone walls, wooden beams, and magnificent views of the lake and the Alps, this beautiful bed and breakfast in a classic Swiss farmhouse oozes rustic elegance.

Each of the five distinctively furnished rooms has comfy mattresses, private bathrooms, and cosy terraces with spectacular views. Guests may rest in the communal living room with a fireplace, cool off in the outdoor pool, or rest on the sun terrace with panoramic views.

The welcoming hosts of Le Petit Verger are enthusiastic about sharing their love of the area and ensuring that tourists enjoy a wonderful stay. They give personalised suggestions for seeing the area's sights, help with transportation and activities, and provide a great breakfast every day that includes fresh local vegetables and handmade delicacies.

4. Le Bleu Léman

Le Bleu Léman, located only steps from the beaches of Lake Geneva, provides a beautiful combination of contemporary amenities and lakeside calm. With large rooms, private balconies, and spectacular lake views, this delightful bed & breakfast in a recently refurbished structure oozes modern elegance.

The six attractively appointed rooms each have comfy mattresses, separate bathrooms, and cosy lounge spaces. Guests may chill in the communal living room with a fireplace, swim in the outdoor pool, or rest on the sun terrace with views of the lake and the Alps.

The welcoming hosts of Le Bleu Léman are dedicated to making visitors' stays unforgettable. They give personalised suggestions for seeing the region's sights, help with transportation and activities, and provide a great breakfast every day that includes fresh local vegetables and handmade delights.

5. Chalet de la Colline

Chalet de la Colline, perched on a mountainside above Montreux, provides a calm respite among stunning views. With exposed wood panelling, cosy fireplaces, and magnificent views of the lake and the Alps, this beautiful bed and breakfast in a classic Swiss chalet oozes rustic elegance.

Each of the five distinctively furnished rooms has a comfy bed, a private bathroom and a cosy balcony with a wonderful view. Guests may rest in the communal living room with a fireplace, cool off in the outdoor pool, or rest on the sun terrace with panoramic views.

The welcoming hosts of Chalet de la Colline are enthusiastic about sharing their love of the area and ensuring that tourists have a wonderful stay. They give personalised suggestions for seeing the area's sites, help with transportation and activities, and provide a great breakfast every day.

Budget-Friendly Hostels for Backpackers

Montreux, a charming lakeside town nestle amidst the breathtaking scenery of the Swiss Riviera, offers a delightful array of budget-friendly hostels that cater to backpackers and budget-conscious travelers. These hostels provide comfortable accommodations, social spaces, and shared facilities, making them an ideal choice for those seeking an affordable and immersive travel experience.

1. Auberge de Jeunesse Montreux
Located just steps from the shores of Lake Geneva, Auberge de Jeunesse Montreux offers a tranquil escape with stunning lake views. This modern hostel features comfortable beds in shared dormitories, private bathrooms, and a spacious common area with a fireplace and a kitchen. Guests can enjoy a refreshing dip in the outdoor pool, relax on the sun terrace, or socialise with fellow travellers in the shared lounge.

2. HI Montreux Youth Hostel
Nestled in the heart of Montreux's old town, HI Montreux Youth Hostel provides a central location for exploring the town's attractions. This historic hostel, housed in a former monastery, features

MONTREUX TRAVEL GUIDE 2024

comfortable beds in shared dormitories, private bathrooms, and a cosy common area with a fireplace and a kitchen. Guests can enjoy a tranquil atmosphere in the shared lounge or socialise with fellow travelers in the outdoor courtyard.

3. Base Montreux
Located just a short walk from the train station, Base Montreux offers a convenient base for exploring the region. This modern hostel features comfortable beds in shared dormitories, private bathrooms, and a spacious common area with a bar, a kitchen, and a game room. Guests can enjoy a lively atmosphere in the shared lounge, unwind in the outdoor terrace, or participate in organised social events and activities.

4. Hostel Funky Monkey Montreux
Hostel Funky Monkey Montreux, located in the centre of Montreux's nightlife zone, provides a dynamic environment for budget-conscious travellers. This contemporary hostel has comfortable beds in sharing dorms, private toilets and a large common area with a bar, kitchen and gaming room. Guests may enjoy live music events in the hostel's own bar, mingle with other travellers in the communal lounge, or take part in organised social events and activities.

5. Youth Hostel Montreux City

Nestled in a quiet neighborhood just a short walk from the lake, Youth Hostel Montreux City offers a peaceful retreat for backpackers. This modern hostel features comfortable beds in shared dormitories, private bathrooms, and a spacious common area with a kitchen and a lounge. Guests can relax in the tranquil garden, enjoy a barbecue area, or socialise with fellow travellers in the shared lounge.

These budget-friendly hostels offer a comfortable and affordable home away from home for backpackers and budget-conscious travelers exploring the enchanting town of Montreux and its breathtaking surroundings. With their convenient locations, shared facilities, and social atmospheres, these hotels provide the perfect base for an unforgettable Swiss adventure.

Unique Stays(Chalets and Airbnb Experiences)

Montreux, a picturesque lakeside town located in the magnificent beauty of the Swiss Riviera, provides a wonderful selection of one-of-a-kind hotels, ranging from classic chalets to contemporary Airbnb experiences, all of which provide an immersive and authentic travel experience.

1. Chalet Le Refuge
Chalet Le Refuge, perched on a mountainside above Montreux, provides a calm haven among stunning landscape. With exposed wood panelling, cosy fireplaces, and breathtaking views of the lake and the Alps, this historic Swiss house oozes rustic appeal.

The chalet has three bedrooms, two bathrooms, and a large living and dining space with a fireplace. Guests may relax on the chalet's balconies and take in the beautiful views, or they can make meals in the fully furnished kitchen.

2. Chalet La Roseraie,
Chalet La Roseraie, set in a quiet rose garden, provides a romantic retreat with a touch of Swiss flair. This classic chalet has a warm and appealing

MONTREUX TRAVEL GUIDE 2024

environment thanks to a mix of old furniture and contemporary comforts.

The chalet has two bedrooms, one bathroom, and a large living and eating space with a fireplace. Guests may relax in the tranquil rose garden, rest in the inviting sitting room, or make meals in the fully equipped kitchen.

3. Chalet Beau Site,
Chalet Beau Site, located only steps from the beaches of Lake Geneva, provides a tranquil escape with spectacular lake views. This contemporary cottage boasts big rooms, private balconies, and breathtaking lakeside views.

The chalet has four bedrooms, three bathrooms, a large living room with a fireplace, a kitchen, and a dining space. Guests may relax on the lakeside patio, chill in the comfortable sitting room, or cook meals in the fully equipped kitchen.

4. Montreux Lakeside Retreat Airbnb Experience
Immerse yourself in Montreux's tranquillity at this beautiful Airbnb experience situated only steps from the shoreline. This contemporary apartment has huge rooms, private balconies, and breathtaking lake views.

The apartment has two bedrooms, one bathroom, a large living room with a fireplace, a kitchen, and a dining area, and a balcony. Guests may relax on the lakeside balcony, chill in the cosy sitting room, or cook in the fully equipped kitchen.

5. Montreux Mountain Chalet Airbnb Experience
This Airbnb experience, hidden among stunning alpine scenery, offers the rustic charm of a classic Swiss house. This cosy cottage has wood panelling, cosy fireplaces, and breathtaking Alps views.

The chalet has three bedrooms, two bathrooms, and a large living and dining space with a fireplace. Guests may relax on the balconies of the chalet, rest in the cosy living room, or make meals in the fully equipped kitchen.

These one-of-a-kind stays provide a remarkable and immersive experience for visitors looking to connect with the beauty and culture of Montreux and its environs. From historic chalets to contemporary Airbnb experiences, these lodgings provide a taste of Swiss hospitality as well as the opportunity to make unforgettable memories.

CRAFTING THE PERFECT ITINERARY

Day 1: Lakeside Promenada Exploration

Morning:

Begin your day with a walk along the gorgeous Lakeside Promenade, which meanders along the shores of Lake Geneva. Take in the breathtaking vistas of Lake Geneva, the magnificent Alps, and the beautiful town of Montreux.

Visit the Freddie Mercury Statue, a bronze memorial to the Queen vocalist, who lived in Montreux in his last years. Take a minute to ponder on his songs and legacy while relaxing by the lake.

Continue on your journey to the Flower Clock, a brightly coloured watch embellished with vivid blossoms. Admire the delicate intricacies and admire the commitment to preserving this blooming beauty.

MONTREUX TRAVEL GUIDE 2024

Lunch:

Enjoy a delicious meal at one of the numerous eateries that along the Lakeside Promenade. Choose from a range of cuisines, ranging from traditional Swiss dishes to cosmopolitan pleasures, all while taking in the stunning lake views.

Afternoon:

Embark on a tour to the Château de Chillon, a medieval fortification set on a rocky island in the lake. Explore the castle's towers, dungeons, and vast halls, as well as its fascinating history and stories.

Take a relaxing boat trip on Lake Geneva, drifting over the calm waters and appreciating the beautiful surroundings. Enjoy the breathtaking vistas of the surrounding mountains and beautiful lakeside village.

Evening:

Enjoy a delicious supper at one of Montreux's well-known restaurants. Enjoy traditional Swiss meals as well as foreign delights at the town's thriving culinary scene.

Immerse yourself in the magical ambiance of Montreux's Jazz Café, a renowned institution that has hosted jazz legends throughout the years. Take in live music performances, take up the bustling atmosphere, and feel the best of the town's musical tradition.

Day 2: Outdoor Adventures in the Swiss Alps

Morning:

Set off on a thrilling walk to the summit of Rochers de Naye, a high peak with panoramic views of Lake Geneva, the Alps and the surrounding area. Enjoy the exhilarating climb and the breathtaking views from the peak.

Take an exciting journey up the hillside on the Montreux-Rochers-de-Naye cogwheel train, a historic railway. Admire the magnificent countryside and revel in the nostalgic appeal of this one-of-a-kind means of transportation.

MONTREUX TRAVEL GUIDE 2024

Discover the Alpine Garden at Rochers de Naye, a biodiversity hotspot with over 6,000 plant species from all over the globe. Explore the perfectly designed gardens and learn about the various flora of the Alpine area.

Lunch:

Enjoy a delectable meal at the Restaurant Le Coucou de Naye, which is set above the Rochers de Naye. While surrounded by stunning surroundings, take in the panoramic views and delight in traditional Swiss cuisine.

Afternoon:

Visit Glacier 3000, a neighbouring Alpine resort with a choice of outdoor activities. Depending on the season, take a spectacular cable car journey to the glacier, where you may enjoy glacier trekking, ice skating, and snow sports.

Glacier 3000's beanie run offers the pleasure of sledding. Descend the twisting path, savouring the thrilling ride and the breathtaking vistas of the surrounding mountains.

Take a guided glacier tour to learn about glacier development and movement. Discover more about these natural beauties and their significance in the Alpine ecology.

Evening:

Return to Montreux and indulge in one of the city's luxury spa resorts. Indulge in revitalising treatment, relax in saunas and steam rooms, and leave feeling revitalised and renewed.

Savour the flavours of classic Swiss cuisine or foreign delicacies at one of Montreux's famous restaurants.

Finish your day with a leisurely walk down the Lakeside Promenade, soaking in the magnificent twilight vistas and lively ambiance of the town.

Day 3: Culinary Delights in Montreux

Morning:

Begin your day in the colourful Montreux Farmers Market, a delightful centre of local produce, artisanal items, and gastronomic treasures. Mix with the people, sample fresh fruits and cheeses, and discover handcrafted specialties while immersing yourself in the lively atmosphere.

Join a guided food tour of Montreux, led by a passionate local guide who will unearth hidden culinary gems and introduce you to the town's rich gastronomic history. Enjoy classic Swiss dishes while learning about the region's culinary traditions and discovering the stories behind the flavours.

Enjoy a delectable brunch at one of Montreux's lovely cafés, enjoying fresh patties, scented coffee, and magnificent lake views. Soak in the bright ambience while enjoying a delicious start to your day.

Afternoon:

Enter the world of Swiss chocolate at the renown Cailler Chocolate Factory, where you'll embark on a wonderful journey of sweet indulgence. Take a guided tour of the plant, learn about the manufacturing process, and indulge in delectable chocolate sampling. Discover the secrets behind Cailler's exquisite creations and learn about the history of Swiss chocolate manufacturing.

Join a scenic wine tasting trip through the vineyards of the Lavaux region, a UNESCO World Heritage Site known for its picturesque terraces and world-class wines. Discover this region's distinct terroir and learn about traditional winemaking techniques. While enjoying the breathtaking views of Lake Geneva and the majestic Alps, savour the flavours of local vintages, including the famed Chasselas and Pinot Noir grapes.

Indulge in the exuberant atmosphere of the Montreux Jazz Café, a legendary venue that has hosted jazz greats throughout its existence. Enjoy live music performances, take up the lively atmosphere, and feel the best of the town's musical history.

Evening:

Enjoy a typical Swiss fondue dinner at one of Montreux's cosy restaurants, where you'll savour melted cheese fondu paired with a variety of dipping ingredients. Enjoy this traditional Swiss cuisine while listening to live folk music and dancing.

End your culinary adventure with a delectable dessert at one of Montreux's well-known pâtisseries. Indulge in exquisite pastries, handcrafted chocolates, and decadent treats to round off your day of gourmet adventures.

Take a leisurely walk down the enchanting Lakeside Promenade, where you can absorb in the enchanting night lights and the dynamic atmosphere of the town. Reflect on the many gastronomic experiences you've had during the day as you stroll, appreciating the rich flavours and traditions Montreux has to offer.

Day 4: Off-the-Beaten-Path Discoveries

Explore beyond the well-trodden tourist paths to find the hidden beauties just beyond Montreux's busy hub. Sét off on an adventure, immersing yourself in the original charm and lesser-known sights that make this area so appealing.

Morning:

Escape to Chexbres, a peaceful town hidden among the undulating vineyards of the Lavaux area. Stroll around the quaint cobblestone lanes, appreciate the classic architecture, and take in the stunning views of Lake Geneva and the Alps.

Explore the vineyards of the Dézaley region, a UNESCO World Heritage Site known for its terraced vines and gorgeous vistas. Enjoy the stroll, see the natural beauty of the area, and immerse yourself in the tranquillity of the countryside.

Visit the Château de Villette, a mediaeval fortress set on a hill with a view of Chexbres. Explore the castle's towers and dungeons, learn about its fascinating history, and take in the breathtaking views of the neighbouring vineyards and Lake Geneva.

Enjoy a delicious lunch at one of Chexbres' beautiful restaurants, savouring traditional Swiss cuisine while admiring the scenic lake and mountain vistas.

Afternoon:

Explore Blonay, a charming town hidden among the green hills of the Chablais area. Discover the nooks of the town, appreciate the old cottages decked with flower displays, and relax in the peaceful ambiance.

Take a guided tour of the Maison du Gruyère, a historic cheese making business where you will learn about the creation of the famous Gruyère cheese. Witness the traditional procedures used to make this world-renowned cheese and have a delicious sampling.

Explore Gruyères, a mediaeval village set on a hill with magnificent views of the surrounding landscape. Stroll around the lovely streets, view the castle and old buildings, and learn about the town's fascinating history, which includes its ties to the Counts of Gruyères.

Explore the adjacent Moléson Nature Reserve, a sanctuary for nature lovers. Hike through the lush woods, marvel at the various flora and wildlife, and take in the crisp mountain air.

Ascend the cable car to the summit of the Moléson Peak for a stunning 360-degree view of the Alps, Lake Geneva, and the surrounding countryside.

Evening:

Return to Montreux via the Moléson Peak, taking in the sunset views of the Alps and Lake Geneva.

Finish your day of off-the-beaten-path explorations with a delicious supper at one of Montreux's famous restaurants, where you can savour the flavours of traditional Swiss cuisine or foreign delicacies. Consider the hidden treasures you've discovered, admiring the true charm and lesser-known attractions that have enhanced your Montreux experience.

Day 5: Relaxation and Spa Day

Morning:

Try a refreshing spa treatment at one of Montreux's opulent spa resorts. Relax in saunas and steam rooms, then indulge yourself with massages and facials to feel refreshed and revitalised.

Take a leisurely walk along the lovely Lakeside Promenade, taking in the tranquil lake views and the colourful town atmosphere. Enjoy the calm wind, drink up the sun, and let the serenity of your surroundings wash over you.

Afternoon:

Enjoy a delectable lunch in one of Montreux's beautiful cafés, where you can savour fresh pastries, fragrant coffee, and breathtaking lake views. Relax in the warm surroundings, absorb in the bright atmosphere, and relax after your spa treatments.

Escape to the quiet Lakeside Gardens, a calm sanctuary in the middle of town. Stroll around the perfectly designed gardens, observe the vibrant blossoms, and relax in the tranquil setting. Take a minute to unwind by the lake, drink up the sun, and let the peace wash over you.

Enjoy a relaxing afternoon tea at one of Montreux's exquisite hotels, savouring delicate sandwiches, pastries, and aromatic teas. After your spa treatments, relax in the sophisticated ambiance and take in the quiet setting.

Evening:

Take a romantic cruise on Lake Geneva, drifting over the calm waters and appreciating the breathtaking sunset vistas. Enjoy the intimate setting, a delectable supper on board, and make great memories among the magnificent lakeside backdrop.

End your relaxing day with a delectable meal at one of Montreux's famous restaurants, savouring the flavours of traditional Swiss cuisine or foreign delicacies. Enjoy the tranquillity of the evening, and let the day's pampering activities to continue to improve your well-being.

OUTDOOR ACTIVITIES

Hiking Trails with Breathtaking Views

Montreux, located in the gorgeous backdrop of the Swiss Riviera, provides a plethora of hiking routes that reveal amazing panoramic views of Lake Geneva, the majestic Alps, and the lovely town itself. Montreux's paths appeal to all skills and interests, whether you're an expert hiker searching for demanding ascents or a leisurely walker looking for lovely strolls.

1. Peak Trail of Rochers-de-Naye: Set off on an unforgettable adventure to the top of Rochers-de-Naye, a high peak with panoramic views of the area. Take the picturesque Montreux-Glion cogwheel train to Caux and then the well-kept route to the summit. You'll pass through beautiful meadows, alpine vegetation, and breathtaking landscapes that will take your breath away.

2. Panorama Path: The Panorama Trail is a somewhat difficult walk that snakes its way through the vineyards of Lavaux, a UNESCO World Heritage Site. As you climb, you'll be rewarded

with breathtaking views of Lake Geneva, the Alps, and the beautiful towns dotting the terrain.

3. The Pèlerin Path: Enjoy the serenity of the Le Pèlerin Trail, a peaceful walk through the beautiful woods and undulating hills of the Chablais area. Enjoy the tranquil setting, listen to nature's calming sounds, and see the wildflowers that line the route.

4. Trail du Col de Sonloup: Begin your trek to the Col de Sonloup, a mountain pass with panoramic views of the surrounding peaks and valleys. The walk leads you through alpine meadows, past flowing waterfalls, and to the top, where you'll be rewarded with stunning views.

5. Lakeside Trail Montreux-Glion: Take a walk along the Montreux-Glion Lakeside Trail, a scenic trail that follows the beaches of Lake Geneva. As you stroll, take in the beautiful lake vistas, appreciate the attractive lakeside villages, and absorb in the quiet mood.

These hiking routes provide a one-of-a-kind chance to see the natural beauty of Montreux and its surrounds. These routes appeal to hikers of all abilities, with varied degrees of difficulty and attractive scenery, providing a memorable and gratifying experience among the stunning surroundings of the Swiss Riviera.

Water Sports on Lake Geneva

Lake Geneva, set among the stunning surroundings of the Swiss Riviera, provides a plethora of water activities, converting the peaceful waters into a playground for thrill seekers and leisure aficionados alike. Whether you're looking for adrenaline-pumping sports or relaxing water-based pleasures, Lake Geneva has something for everyone.

1. SUP (stand-up paddleboarding): Glide over the calm waters of Lake Geneva on a stand-up paddleboard, taking in the scenery and working out. SUP allows you to paddle at your own speed and discover coves and shorelines, giving you a unique view of the surroundings.

2. Windsurfing: Windsurfing allows you to harness the strength of the wind and ride the waves of Lake Geneva. The excitement of gliding over the water, the difficulty of balancing and manoeuvring the board, and the ecstasy of capturing the wind's force are all part of the experience.

3. Canoeing and Kayaking: Explore Lake Geneva's tranquil coves and gorgeous inlets at your own speed in a kayak or canoe. Paddle along calm waterways surrounded by stunning landscape, and enjoy the peace and closeness to nature.

4. Waterskiing and wakeboarding: Feel the exhilaration of waterskiing or wakeboarding while cutting explosive curves behind a fast boat. Enjoy the excitement of gliding at great speed over the water, the struggle of keeping balance and control, and the pleasure of the rise.

5. Sailing: Enjoy the peace and beauty of sailing on Lake Geneva. Set sail among the breathtaking landscape, enjoy the mild wind and the boat's rhythmic swing, and immerse yourself in the tranquil ambiance of the lake.

6. Scuba Diving and Snorkelling: Discover Lake Geneva's underwater realm, which is home to a rich diversity of fish and aquatic life. Explore the lake's depths, marvel at the beautiful underwater scenery, and meet the strange animals that live in this secret world.

7. Whitewater Rafting: Whitewater rafting on the Rhône River, which feeds into Lake Geneva, is a

thrilling experience. Navigate over difficult rapids as a team, and enjoy the thrilling ride among the stunning surroundings of the river valley.

8. Pedalo Boating: A delightful and peaceful activity for families and parties is a leisurely pedalo boat trip on Lake Geneva. Pedal at your own speed, absorb in the sun and lake views, and relax in the peaceful setting.

9 Jet Skiing: Feel the rush of excitement as you sprint over the surface of the lake on a jet ski. Feel the adrenaline of high-speed manoeuvres, the pleasure of navigating vast seas, and the wind in your hair.

10. Flyboarding: Flyboarding, a unique activity that combines aspects of water jetpacking and snowboarding, will elevate your water sports experience. Launch yourself into the air, execute gravity-defying acrobatics, and take in the beautiful vistas from above.

11. Parasailing: From the vantage point of a parasail, soar over the lake and enjoy panoramic views of Montreux and its surrounds. Feel the rush of being lifted into the air, the peace of gliding over water, and the beautiful views from above.

12. Waterskiing Instruction: Take advantage of waterskiing classes provided at several sites around Lake Geneva, whether you're a novice or an experienced skier trying to improve your technique. Learn the basics, put your abilities to the test, and experience the excitement of gliding over the water under professional supervision.

13. Wakeboarding Instruction: Experience the thrill of wakeboarding with the assistance of skilled instructors. Learn the fundamentals, hone your balance and control, and enjoy the excitement of carving turns and surfing a boat's wake.

14. Sailing Courses: Accept the art of sailing and learn to traverse the seas of Lake Geneva. Enrol in sailing classes at local sailing schools to learn the foundations of sailing, boat handling, and manoeuvring methods.

15. Kayak Tours with a Guide: A guided kayak trip of Lake Geneva will allow you to discover secret coves and lovely inlets. Paddle alongside knowledgeable guides while learning about the lake's biology and history, and discovering hidden jewels along the route.

16. Scuba Diving Courses: Scuba diving training will take you on a voyage into the underwater world of Lake Geneva. Discover the intriguing underwater environment under the lake's surface by learning the principles of scuba diving, safety procedures, and underwater exploration skills.

These water activities provide exciting experiences, calm getaways, and chances to connect with nature, allowing a range of ways to appreciate the beauty and tranquillity of Lake Geneva. Lake Geneva provides something for everyone, whether you're looking for adrenaline-fueled thrills, peaceful water-based pleasures, or chances to learn and develop your talents.

Skiing and Snowboarding in the Nearby

1. Les Diablerets: Les Diablerets, nestle among the breathtaking peaks of the Vaud Alps, is a famous ski resort that offers a thrilling winter paradise for snow sports aficionados. Les Diablerets, with over 120 km of varied ski courses, appeals to skiers and snowboarders of all abilities, from novices looking for moderate slopes to seasoned thrill-seekers looking for demanding off-piste excursions. The breathtaking views of the neighbouring

snow-capped mountains and the lovely valley below enhance the enthralling experience.

2. Villars-Gryon: Villars-Gryon is the ideal place for a family-friendly ski resort with a quiet ambiance and a choice of activities for all ages. Villars-Gryon delivers a safe and pleasurable skiing experience for novices and families, with over 120 km of well-groomed slopes. A special beginner's section at the resort, complete with soft slopes and attentive instructors, guarantees an introduction to the world of skiing. Explore the resort's various terrain as you go, including demanding off-piste experiences for skilled skiers. When you're not on the slopes, enjoy the resort's attractive environment, which includes cosy restaurants, scenic chalets, and a range of après-ski activities.

3. Leysin: Enjoy the panoramic views and sun-kissed slopes of Lysine, a ski resort noted for its superb snow conditions and varied terrain. Leysin caters to skiers and snowboarders of all abilities, with over 65 km of ski lines providing both easy slopes for beginners and difficult off-piste excursions for specialists. The resort's famed freestyle park, with its assortment of jumps and rails, is a playground for adrenaline junkies, while the well-kept slopes provide a serene retreat for

those looking for a more leisurely skiing experience. You'll enjoy Leysin's unique combination of exciting terrain and tranquil environment as you take in the breathtaking views of the surrounding mountains and the gorgeous valley below.

4. Glacier 3000: For an extraordinary skiing experience that extends beyond the conventional winter season, visit Glacier 3000, a one-of-a-kind ski resort that offers year-round skiing and stunning glacier vistas. Ascend via cable car to the glacier's crest, where you'll be welcomed with a panoramic view of snow-capped peaks and beautiful alpine scenery. Even in the summer, almost 25 km of groomed slopes await, delivering a tough but rewarding skiing experience. Discover the glacier's unique landscape, such as crevasses and snow bridges, and experience the thrill of gliding on the endless ice.

5. Soleil Portes: Set off on a cross-border skiing excursion in Portes du Soleil, a resort shared by Switzerland and France. Portes du Soleil, with over 650 km of linked ski routes, provides an unrivalled skiing experience for skiers and snowboarders of all abilities. Explore the varied terrain, which includes easy slopes for beginners as well as difficult off-piste excursions for specialists. The resort's

unique cross-border element enables you to ski in two nations in a single day, allowing you to experience the contrasting flavours and cultures of Switzerland and France while you glide down the slopes.

Montreux's ski resorts cater to a broad variety of interests and ability levels, whether you're looking for the excitement of demanding slopes, the peace of mild runs, or the beauty of family-friendly activities. These resorts deliver an extraordinary winter trip, generating memories that will last a lifetime, with great snow conditions, diversified terrain, and magnificent alpine scenery.

Paragliding Adventures Over Montreux

Soar the picturesque town of Montreux and take in the spectacular splendour of the Swiss Riviera from a new viewpoint. Paragliding above Montreux is a one-of-a-kind and spectacular opportunity to interact with the region's natural beauty, generating experiences that will last a lifetime.

1. Tandem paragliding: Experience the excitement of tandem paragliding, an excellent choice for individuals wanting an unforgettable experience

but lacking previous paragliding expertise. You'll softly glide over the stunning surroundings with an experienced and qualified pilot, taking in panoramic views of Lake Geneva, the magnificent Alps, and the lovely town of Montreux. Your skilled pilot will guide you through the air currents and share their expertise of the region's stunning surroundings to guarantee a safe and pleasurable ride.

2. Solo paragliding: Solo paragliding above Montreux provides an unrivalled challenge for skilled paragliders looking for the ultimate solo adventure. Ascend into the immense expanse of the sky from certified launch locations, led by qualified instructors. Experience the sheer pleasure of solo flying while navigating the air currents and viewing the spectacular scenery from a unique viewpoint.

3. Thermal paragliding: In an amazing thermal paragliding journey, harness the natural force of thermals, warm air currents that propel paragliders to greater heights. Ascend above Montreux with your professional pilot, taking in panoramic views of the region's gorgeous surroundings. Learn to recognise and use natural updrafts to increase your flight duration and reach new heights as you fly through the skies.

4. Cross-Country Paragliding: Explore the varied landscapes of the Swiss Riviera from the skies on an amazing cross-country paragliding adventure. Travel over the region's green valleys, beautiful mountains, and lovely towns with your skilled pilot. Immerse yourself in the tranquillity of the flight, soaking in the gorgeous scenery and the exhilaration of reaching huge distances while flying through the skies.

5. Paragliding at Sunrise and Sunset: Witness the stunning shift of the landscape while paragliding above Montreux at dawn or dusk. Ascend into the skies at sunrise to see the sun paint the Alps in bright colours, throwing a warm light over the surrounding landscape. Alternatively, take in the lovely view of the sunset, as the sky turns colours and the town lights begin to glitter below.

6. Acrobatic paragliding: Acrobatic paragliding is an amazing task for adrenaline junkies. Learn the skills and manoeuvres of acrobatic paragliding with professional instructors, including exhilarating spirals, loops, and wingovers. Feel the surge of excitement as you perform these aerial manoeuvres while admiring the environment from above.

7. Family-Friendly Paragliding Experiences: Even families with little children may enjoy the adrenaline rush of paragliding above Montreux. Many paragliding companies provide tandem flights tailored exclusively for children, offering a safe and entertaining experience for the whole family. Make amazing moments as you soar above the city, soaking in the spectacular vistas and experiencing the pleasure of flight.

8. Photography and Videography of Paragliding: Using photography and film, you may capture the magnificent beauty of your paragliding journey. Many pilots enable you to attach cameras to your harness, enabling you to take beautiful airborne film and panoramic images of the surrounding countryside. Share your unique view of Montreux and the Swiss Riviera with others, leaving them with enduring visual memories of your paragliding adventure.

9. Festivals and Events for Paragliding: Attend one of the numerous festivals and events conducted in the Montreux area throughout the year to immerse yourself in the colourful world of paragliding. These events include contests, demonstrations, and chances to meet and connect with expert pilots,

showcasing the abilities and enthusiasm of paragliders from across the globe.

Paragliding above Montreux provides an unparalleled experience that will leave you breathless and filled with amazement, whether you prefer a leisurely tandem flight, the challenge of solo paragliding, or the exhilaration of aerobatic manoeuvres. You'll get a great appreciation for the marvels of the natural world and the exciting freedom of flight as you fly over the stunning landscapes and view the splendour of the Swiss Riviera from a unique perspective.

ADRENALINE-PUMPING EXPERIENCES

Bungee Jumping from the Verzasca Dam

Bungee leap from the historic Verzasca Dam, a 220-meter-tall structure situated among the stunning beauty of the Swiss Riviera, for the ultimate adrenaline thrill. This iconic bungee jump, immortalised in the James Bond film "GoldenEye," provides an unrivalled thrill-seeking encounter, mixing the rush of freefall with the breathtaking scenery of the Verzasca Valley.

1. Planning and Safety Measures: Before your bungee leap, you'll go through extensive safety tests and training from experienced and qualified jump masters. You'll be equipped with a sturdy harness and double-checked during the jump to guarantee your safety. The jump masters will give you clear instructions and direction to ensure you're ready for the thrilling adventure ahead.

2. Ascension to the Jump Platform: As you go to the jump platform at the top of the Verzasca Dam, take in the amazing views of the Verzasca Valley. As you take in the enormous expanse below, the

flowing waters of the Verzasca River, and the breathtaking peaks of the surrounding mountains, your excitement grows.

3. Leap of Faith: Take a deep breath and prepare for the leap of faith while standing on the edge of the jump platform. The feeling of freefall will take your breath away as you plunge into the nothingness. As you plunge into the valley below, the wind will blow past you, giving you the ultimate adrenaline sensation.

4. The Rebound and Pleasure: As you swing back and forth, the bungee rope will gently catch you and provide an exciting rebound experience. Enjoy the rush of adrenaline, the sensation of weightlessness, and the beautiful vistas that surround you.

5. The Drop and a Safe Landing: As the excitement wears off, the experienced jump masters will gently drop you to the earth. Take a minute to appreciate the success of overcoming your worries and participating in this once-in-a-lifetime trip.

6. The Souvenir and Courage Certificate: Receive a commemorative memento and bravery certificate for successfully bungee jumping from the Verzasca Dam. These mementos will be a constant reminder of your courage and the remarkable experience you've had.

How to Have a Memorable Bungee Jumping Experience:

1. Overcome your worries and approach the problem with optimism.

2. Pay close attention to the jump masters' directions and keep your cool during the exercise.

3. Take in the magnificent grandeur of the Verzasca Valley from the jump platform's unique vantage point.

4. Enjoy the surge of adrenaline and the sensation of freefall.

5. Share your adventures with friends and family, making memories that will last a lifetime.

Bungee jumping from the Verzasca Dam is an amazing event that will leave you feeling energised and buzzed. Conquer your anxieties, enjoy the excitement, and make memories that last a lifetime.

Skydiving with Panoramic Alpine Vistas

Experience the ultimate exhilaration of freefall and the mesmerising beauty of the surrounding mountains on a memorable skydiving trip among the stunning backdrop of the Swiss Alps. Take in the spectacular views of snow-capped peaks, green valleys, and the lovely town of Montreux nestling below as you plummet into the earth.

1. Planning and Safety Measures: Before you begin your skydiving journey, you will be subjected to extensive safety tests and instructions from experienced and licenced instructors. You'll be outfitted with a sturdy harness and parachute, which will keep you safe during the leap. The instructors will give you precise directions and assistance to ensure you're ready for the thrilling adventure ahead.

2. Ascension to Jump Altitude: Board the plane that will take you to the jump height, which is usually approximately 4, 000 metres above earth. Admire the beautiful views of the Swiss Alps, the patchwork of farmland and towns below, and the glistening expanse of Lake Geneva as you rise.

3. The Leap from the Aeroplane: Take a deep breath and prepare to plunge into the great expanse below as you stand at the open door of the aeroplane. Step out into the open air, excitement coursing through your veins, with your expert instructor securely connected.

4. The Thrilling Freefall: Feel the exciting feeling of freefall as you descend to the ground at speeds of up to 200 kilometres per hour. The wind will rush by you, the environment will blur into a flurry of colours, and you will experience a sense of weightlessness.

5. The Parachute's Deployment: Your instructor will deploy the parachute at the specified height, changing the sense of freefall into a smooth drop. The parachute will softly fill, slowing your descent and giving you a calm view of the stunning scenery below.

6. Gliding through Alpine Vistas: Take in the breathtaking views of the Swiss Alps as you fall elegantly. Admire the landscape's snow-capped peaks, green valleys, and beautiful villages. The peaceful environment and spectacular beauty will capture your senses, leaving you with a memorable recollection.

7. The Easy Landing: You'll make a smooth and controlled touchdown on a designated landing place under the supervision of your expert instructor. You will feel a rush of excitement and success as you stand tall, having overcome your anxieties and experienced the ultimate adrenaline rush.

How to Have a Memorable Skydiving Experience:

1. Accept the task and face your anxieties with a positive attitude.

2. Pay close attention to your teachers' directions and keep your cool during the procedure.

3. Use a mounted camera or GoPro to capture the spectacular sights, generating lasting visual memories.

4. Share your experience with friends and family, making memories together.

5. Enjoy the exciting feeling of freefall and the tranquillity of floating across the Alpine scenery.

Skydiving with magnificent mountain landscapes provides an unrivalled blend of adrenaline-pumping thrill and breathtaking beauty. In the middle of the spectacular backdrop of the Swiss Alps, embrace the excitement, overcome your anxieties, and make memories that last a lifetime.

Mountain Biking Trails for Thrill-Seekers

Montreux and its surrounding area have a wide variety of mountain bike tracks to suit both thrill seekers and leisure riders. From demanding off-road experiences to gorgeous cross-country rides, these paths provide a thrilling opportunity to discover the Swiss Riviera's magnificent scenery.

1. Col de Sonloup Trail: Begin your trek to the Col de Sonloup, a mountain pass with panoramic views of the surrounding peaks and valleys. The walk leads you through alpine meadows, past flowing waterfalls, and to the top, where you'll be

rewarded with stunning views. With steep portions, rooty terrain, and technical aspects, the descent delivers an exciting challenge.

2. Montreux-Glion Lakeside Trail: Take a leisurely mountain bike ride along the Montreux-Glion Lakeside Trail, a scenic trail that follows the beaches of Lake Geneva. The path has a combination of mild slopes and modest climbs, making it a picturesque and fun ride for cyclists of all skill levels. Along the journey, you'll pass through attractive lakeside villages, lush woods, and stunning views of the lake and the Alps.

3. Les Rochers-de-Naye Peak Trail: The top of Les Rochers-de-Naye, a high peak accessible by cogwheel train and mountain bike routes, offers a beautiful view of Lake Geneva and the Alps. The path winds through alpine meadows and along the hillside, providing both tough climbs and delightful descents. The views from the peak are absolutely spectacular, making the difficult journey worthwhile.

4. Chablais Panorama Trail: Enjoy the peace and beauty of the Chablais Panorama Trail, a fairly difficult mountain bike ride that weaves through the green hills of the Chablais area. The path has a

diversity of topography, ranging from easy slopes to difficult climbs, and gives breathtaking views of the neighbouring valleys, towns, and Lake Geneva in the distance.

5. Les Diablerets Bike Park: Les Diablerets biking Park, a famous mountain biking destination with a range of downhill routes, flow trails, and jump lines, is a thrill-seekers heaven. The park welcome riders of all skill levels, from novices looking for moderate slopes to expert cyclists looking for demanding terrain. The park's picturesque setting among the towering peaks of the Vaud Alps adds to the thrilling experience.

6. Leysin MTB Trails: Explore the varied terrain of Lysin, a popular mountain biking destination with routes ranging from moderate family rides to difficult cross-country excursions. The paths run through woods, meadows, and along the slope, providing breathtaking vistas as well as a range of difficulties for riders of all skill levels.

7. Villars-Gryon Bike Park: At Villars-Gryon Bike Park, a famous location offering a choice of tough routes for skilled riders, you can feel the excitement of downhill mountain biking. The park's flow tracks provide a fun and exciting ride,

while its jump courses let you to put your abilities to the test and enjoy the ultimate adrenaline rush.

8. Portes du Soleil Bike Area: Explore the huge and varied landscape of Portes du Soleil, a common cross-border biking region shared by Switzerland and France. Portes du Soleil, with over 650 km of interconnecting trails, provides an unrivalled mountain biking experience for riders of all abilities. The area's diverse topography, ranging from easy slopes to tough off-piste excursions, offers a limitless number of possibilities to explore and enjoy the excitement of mountain biking in stunning landscape.

Montreux and its surrounding area provide a broad choice of mountain biking routes that appeal to every inclination and ability level, whether you're looking for the excitement of difficult downhill tracks, the calm of gorgeous cross-country rides, or a combination of both. These paths give an incredible opportunity to enjoy the splendour of the Swiss Riviera while experiencing the adrenaline rush of mountain biking, with magnificent scenery, hard terrain, and a range of alternatives to pick from.

Rock Climbing in the Swiss Riviera

With its towering limestone cliffs, gushing waterfalls, and verdant valleys, the Swiss Riviera provides an unequalled rock climbing paradise for climbers of all abilities, from seasoned veterans to eager newcomers. The area provides a broad choice of climbing routes that suit to every ability level and desire, from the legend ary crags of Montreux to the hidden treasures of the Chablais region.

1. Rochers-de-Naye Climbing Area: Climbers will find a sanctuary on Rochers-de-Naye, a high summit reachable by cogwheel train. The region has a range of single-pitch and multi-pitch routes ranging from simple slabs to difficult overhangs, making it a perfect challenge for climbers of all abilities. The summit's spectacular views of Lake Geneva and the Alps add to the exciting experience.

2. Col de Sonloup Climbing Area: Col de Sonloup, nestle among the gorgeous peaks of the Vaud Alps, provides a unique and hard climbing experience. The region has a range of multi-pitch routes ranging from moderate to demanding, challenging experienced climbers' abilities and stamina. The breathtaking views of the neighbouring valleys, as well as the peace and quiet of the alpine

environment, contribute to the attractiveness of this climbing location.

3. Les Diablerets Climbing Area: Les Diablerets, surrounded by the snow-capped peaks of the Vaud Alps, provides a broad choice of climbing routes, ranging from beginner-friendly slabs to tough multi-pitch excursions. The high altitude of the location gives a cool respite from the summer heat, while the beautiful views of the surrounding mountains make for an amazing climbing experience.

4. Leysin Climbing Area: The Leysin Climbing Area, which overlooks the scenic town of Leysin, provides a choice of single-pitch and multi-pitch routes for climbers of all abilities. The area's easy access, well-maintained paths, and spectacular views of the surrounding valleys make it a popular destination for expert climbers as well as those looking for a softer start to the sport.

5. Montreux Climbing Area: The Montreux Climbing Area, located in the centre of Montreux, provides a handy and accessible choice for climbers of all abilities. The closeness of the location to the town centre makes it simple to combine climbing with other activities, and the range of single-pitch

and multi-pitch routes offers a good challenge for climbers looking for a fast adrenaline hit.

6. Chablais Climbing Area: The Chablais Climbing Area, hidden among the green hills of the Chablais area, provides a calm getaway from the masses, allowing a more personal and intimate climbing experience. The region offers a wide range of single-pitch routes, from simple beginning slabs to difficult overhangs, to climbers of all skill levels.

7. Villars-Gryon Climbing Area: The Villars-Gryon Climbing Area, nestled in the scenic landscape of Villars-Gryon, provides a choice of single-pitch and multi-pitch routes, providing a suitable challenge for climbers of all abilities. The area's well-kept routes, spectacular views of the surrounding mountains, and accessibility to town make it a popular destination for both experienced climbers and visitors looking for a more leisurely climbing experience.

8. Grimsel Pass Climbing Area: The Grimsel Pass Climbing Area provides a range of multi-pitch routes on granite cliffs, presenting a test of endurance and technical abilities to those looking for a unique and demanding climbing experience. The high height of the location, along with

breathtaking views of the surrounding mountains, makes for an outstanding climbing journey.

Whether you're a seasoned climber looking for the excitement of demanding multi-pitch routes or an enthusiastic novice looking to get your feet wet in the world of rock climbing, the Swiss Riviera has a broad choice of climbing possibilities to suit every preference and ability level. The region is a veritable paradise for rock climbing fans, with its magnificent scenery, world-class climbing routes, and inviting climbing community.

NIGHTLIFE AND ENTERTAINMENT

Trendy Bars and Nightclubs in Montreux

Montreux, hidden among the magnificent landscapes of the Swiss Riviera, is known not only for its mesmerising beauty and cultural attractions, but also for its active nightlife scene, which caters to a wide spectrum of tastes and preferences. Montreux provides an exceptional experience for visitors wishing to revel in the town's dynamic ambiance, from refined cocktail bars radiating elegance and sophistication to throbbing nightclubs buzzing with thrilling sounds.

1. Funky Claude's Bar: Funky Claude's Bar, a renowned restaurant inside the Fairmont Le Montreux Palace, welcomes you into the world of classic drinks and timeless elegance. This well-known club is known for its superb service, inventive drink mixes, and lively live music events. Renowned mixologists use fresh ingredients to create a symphony of flavours, making each drink into an art form. Immerse yourself in the bar's enchanting environment as you drink your perfectly crafted libation, where the throbbing rhythms of

live music blend with the intelligent talk of other revellers.

2. Le Millesime Club: At Le Millesime Club, a high-end nightclub that redefines the Montreux nightlife experience, embrace the pinnacle of luxury and extravagance. The pulsing music, trendy setting, and exquisite VIP bottle service lure a discerning audience to this private restaurant. Renowned worldwide DJs produce an exhilarating blend of house, techno, and electronic music, converting the club into a refuge for partygoers and dance fans. Allow the intoxicating rhythms to direct your movements as you immerse yourself in the club's dynamic environment and enjoy the excitement of an incredible night out.

3. Taboo Bar & Lounge: Taboo Bar & Lounge, a classy paradise nestle on the beaches of Lake Geneva, offers an escape from the everyday. This intriguing bar provides a calm haven, with panoramic views of the surrounding mountains and the glistening lake providing a stunning background to your evening. Relax in the sophisticated environment of the bar and savour the broad selection of perfectly created cocktails, each delicately prepared with fresh ingredients and a touch of delicacy. Taboo Bar & Lounge provides an

amazing experience whether you're looking for a pre-dinner drink or a night out with pals.

4. Sunset Bar at Fairmont Le Montreux Palace: At the Sunset Bar, a rooftop sanctuary above the Fairmont Le Montreux Palace, see the enchantment of Montreux sunsets as they paint the sky with bright colours. This stylish bar provides a stunning view of Lake Geneva and the surrounding Alps, creating an atmosphere unlike any other. Allow the stunning sights and soothing sounds of the setting sun to take you to a state of absolute tranquillity as you drink a glass of champagne or a specialty cocktail.

5. La Cucina at the Hôtel Royal: At La Cucina, a hidden treasure inside Hôtel Royal, go on a gastronomic and drink odyssey. Handcrafted drinks and excellent food combine to offer an amazing experience at this classy bar. Allow the professional mixologists to lead you through their comprehensive cocktail menu while you savour the bar's gastronomic wonders, each creation a monument to their love and inventiveness. La Cucina provides a unique gastronomic and drink trip, whether you're looking for a romantic evening or a special occasion party.

6. Le Cristal: Immerse yourself in the exhilarating excitement of Le Cristal, a popular nightclub that has established itself as a fixture of Montreux's bustling nightlife scene. With its throbbing sounds spanning from house and techno to pop and R&B, this energetic venue draws a broad mix of residents and tourists. Allow the vast dance floor and colourful lights to convert the night into a memorable experience as you submit to the seductive rhythms. Le Cristal guarantees an explosive night of dancing and merriment, whether you're a seasoned clubber or a curious novice.

7. Le Loft: Beyond the mainstream, you'll find the hidden jewel that is Le Loft, an underground paradise for alternative music fans. This tiny club draws a laid-back clientele attracted to its varied mix of music, which includes rock, indie, techno, and experimental sounds. Allow the throbbing rhythms of unknown jewels to wash over you as you travel the darkly lighted passageways and cosy surroundings. Le Loft is an ideal environment for a night of musical discovery and socialising with other music lovers.

8. La Maison du Whisky: Whisky connoisseurs will find heaven at La Maison du Whisky, a refuge for whisky enthusiasts of all levels. This little bar offers a diverse range of whiskies from across the globe, as well as expert suggestions and experienced personnel. Allow the soft lighting and intimate ambiance to set the one for an evening of whisky tasting and appreciation as you explore the bar's huge collection. La Maison du Whisky guarantees an amazing trip into the world of whisky, whether you're a seasoned enthusiast or a curious newbie.

Jazz and Music Festivals in the Region

Montreux and its surrounding area have a thriving schedule of jazz and music events, drawing music fans from all over the world. These events provide a one-of-a-kind chance to immerse yourself in the region's rich musical history and the enticing melodies and rhythms of many genres.

1. Montreux Jazz Festival: The Montreux Jazz Festival, held annually in early July, is the world's second-largest annual jazz festival, noted for its eclectic roster of musicians and iconic performances. Every year, about 250, 000 people attend the festival, which features a mix of jazz, blues, gospel, soul, rock, and other popular music genres. The festival turns Montreux into a dynamic

music centre over two weeks, with concerts presented in a variety of locations, including the famous Auditorium Stravinski and the open-air stage at the Lakeside Promenade.

2. Cully Jazz Festival: The Cully Jazz Festival, nestle among the vineyards of the Lavaux area, provides a more intimate and easygoing ambiance, drawing around 60, 000 guests each year. The festival, which takes place in late June, has a broad array of jazz musicians, ranging from old classics to rising stars, and serves as a platform for both famous and new talents. The festival's unusual environment, among the scenic vineyards and lovely hamlet of Cully, contributes to the overall vibe, producing a memorable experience for music fans.

3. Nyon Folk Festival: At the Nyon Folk Festival, held annually in late July, embrace the colourful sounds of folk music. Every year, approximately 50, 000 people attend this famous festival, which showcases a varied spectrum of folk music from throughout the globe, from classic melodies to modern adaptations. The open-air stages and smaller locations of the festival create a setting where music and nature merge, resulting in a

harmonic combination of cultural expressions among Nyon's stunning scenery.

4. Estival de Musique de Fribourg: The Estival de Musique de Fribourg, held annually in July and August, has an unusual blend of genres. This famous festival, which attracts over 20, 000 guests each year, features a varied spectrum of musical genres, from classical to jazz, rock, and world music. The festival's distinct atmosphere, which combines the old city of Fribourg with contemporary performance venues, provides an enthralling setting for musical discovery.

5. Paleo Festival Nyon: Immerse yourself in the thrilling atmosphere of the Paleo Festival Nyon, which takes place every year in July. Every year, approximately 230, 000 people attend this famous event, which has a broad roster of international musicians ranging from rock and pop to techno and world music. The festival's six open-air stages and energetic atmosphere convert Nyon into a throbbing hive of music and merriment, providing festivalgoers with an unparalleled experience.

6. Les Heures du Jazz à Villars-Gryon: Throughout the summer, Les Heures du Jazz à Villars-Gryon hosts a series of private jazz performances. This

delightful jazz festival draws jazz fans searching for a more casual and personal environment, with a variety of concerts in the cost venues of Villars-Gryon, a scenic mountain hamlet overlooking the Rhone Valley.

7. Jazz sur les Toits: Jazz sur les Toits, held yearly in July and August, is a one-of-a-kind blend of jazz and architecture. This unique event converts Montreux's roofs into open-air stages, displaying a range of jazz acts against the breathtaking skyline of the town. The festival's distinct atmosphere, which combines jazz's rhythmic melodies with Montreux's beautiful surroundings, produces a memorable experience for music fans.

8. Jazz à Thônex: Celebrate Thônex's thriving jazz culture at the Jazz à Thônex festival, held each September. This famous event attracts over 30, 000 guests each year and has a broad array of jazz musicians ranging from known veterans to budding talents. The festival's many stages and small settings offer a platform for musical exploration and discovery, providing jazz fans with a remarkable experience.

Casino Montreux(Gaming and Glamour)

Casino Montreux is an iconic symbol of luxury, entertainment, and gaming excitement, nestled among the magnificent surroundings of the Swiss Riviera. The casino has attracted guests from all over the world with its sumptuous decor, world-class gaming facilities, and a long history of spectacular performances since its initial debut in 1954.

A Glamour and Entertainment Legacy

You'll be transported into a world of sophisticated elegance and enthralling entertainment the minute you walk through the majestic entryway of Casino Montreux. The sumptuous decor of the casino, along with shimmering chandeliers and complex architectural features, gets the one for an amazing experience. The vivid sounds of roulette wheels spinning, chips clinking, and slot machines buzzing will fill the air as you explore the expansive gaming floors, producing a real feeling of excitement and expectation.

A World of Exciting Gaming Possibilities

Casino Montreux has a wide variety of gaming opportunities to suit every taste and style. Whether you're an experienced gambler or a first-time visitor, the casino's large assortment of table games, slot machines, and electronic gaming alternatives will keep you entertained and excited for hours. Immerse yourself in the excitement of traditional table games like roulette, blackjack, and poker, or try your luck on the fascinating wheels of slot machines, each of which offers the possibility of a life-changing prize.

A Culinary Retreat with Live Entertainment

Aside from the thrills of the gambling floors, Casino Montreux offers a choice of gastronomic pleasure to tempt your taste buds. The casino caters to every palette and eating choice, with everything from fine dining venues providing great food to informal pubs and cafés selling wonderful snacks and drinks.

The casino evolves into a centre of live entertainment as the evening advances, featuring enthralling performances by famous musicians, dancers, and magicians. Whether you are looking for the exciting rhythms of live music or the stunning artistry of stage acts, Casino Montreux will provide you with an amazing evening of entertainment.

A Musical Legends Tribute

Casino Montreux has a particular place in the hearts of music fans throughout the globe, having staged iconic concerts by legends such as Quincy Jones, Ella Fitzgerald, and David Bowie. The epic "Deep Purple in Concert" performance, which was documented on the band's famed live album "Made in Japan, " solidified the casino's status as a platform for spectacular musical events.

A Must-See Location

Casino Montreux is more than simply a gambling establishment; it embodies beauty, entertainment, and a rich cultural past. Whether you're looking for the thrill of the gaming tables, the appeal of live entertainment, or a gastronomic experience that will tantalise your taste buds, Casino Montreux guarantees an extraordinary voyage into the world of luxury and excitement.

LOCAL CUISINE

Swiss Fondue(A Culinary Must-Try)

Set off on a gastronomic adventure with Swiss fondue, a quintessential meal that has captivated palats all over the globe with its creamy, cheesy goodness. This classic Alpine dish was created in the Swiss highlands as a simple and satisfying meal for shepherds and farmers. Fondue has evolved into a national treasure throughout the centuries, becoming a symbol of Swiss culture and hospitality.

A Flavour and Texture Symphony

The essence of Swiss fondue lies in its simplicity and perfect flavour blend. A blend of melted cheeses, generally a mix of Gruyère and Emmental, two Swiss cheeses renowned for their rich, creamy textures and nutty notes, sits at the heart of this meal. As the cheeses meet together in a shared pot, they form a velvety, gooey combination that is both soothing and irresistible.

The Dipping and Savouring Art

Fondue's true delight lies in the social experience of sharing and savouring. Gather around the fondue pot, armed with bread cubes, charcuterie, or boiled vegetables. Dip your chosen morsels slowly into the boiling cheese, allowing them to get generously coated with the rich, savoury fondue. Let the symphony of flavours dance on your tongue as you savour the first bite, the creamy cheese blending with the subtle notes of the bread or the earth flavours of the vegetables.

A Culinary Experiment with Variations

While classic fondue asks for a blend of Gruyère and Emmental cheeses, there are several alternatives to try. Moitié-Moitié fondue is made with equal parts Gruyèrre and Vacherin, resulting in a somewhat sweeter and milder flavour. Try fondue neuchâteloise, a blend of Vacherin and Tête de Moine famed for its somewhat tangy and spicy notes, for a bolder taste.

Beyond the Cheese: Accompaniments and Beverages

While the melted cheese is the star of the show, fondue is often accompanied by a variety of side dishes to round out the flavours. Cornichons, or pickled cucumbers, provide a refreshing counterpoint to the richness of the cheese, while boiled potatoes provide a hearty and fulfilling complement. A squeeze of lemon juice or a splash of white wine may add a touch of acidity to the flavours.

Consider a glass of classic Swiss wine to go with your fondue experience. Fendant, a light and fruity white wine, is a traditional choice, while Pinot Noir, with its subtle notches, rounds out the richness of the cheese. A glass of bubbling mineral water is a refreshing palate cleanser that is non-alcoholic.

An Enduring Culinary Tradition

Swiss fondue has evolved from humble beginnings to become a culinary classic, a symbol of Swiss culture and hospitality. Its enduring appeal stems from its simplicity, capacity to bring people together, and the thrill of savouring the rich, creamy goodness of melted cheese. Gather your friends and family, gather around the fondue pot, and go on a gastronomic adventure that will leave you with unforgettable memories.

Traditional Alpine Dishes

Montreux, nestled among the magnificent vistas of the Swiss Riviera, is a gastronomic sanctuary for visitors seeking classic Alpine delicacies. The region's food reflects the spirit of Alpine cuisine, highlighting the rich flavours and nutritious ingredients that have been handed down through centuries, from substantial cheese-based delicacies to savoury meat meals.

1. Raclette: Raclette, a meal that has become associated with Swiss cuisine, is the pinnacle of Alpine luxury. Melted raclette cheese, a semi-hard cheese with a rich, buttery flavour, is scraped over boiling potatoes, charcuterie, and pickled vegetables in this classic meal. As the cheese pours over your selected accompaniments, you'll have a savoury concoction that's both soothing and tempting.

2. Rösti: Discover the simplicity and pleasant flavours of rösti, a traditional Swiss meal that highlights the region's fondness for potatoes. Pan-fry shredded potatoes until golden brown, creating a crispy surface that gives way to a soft and fluffy inside. Rösti is often served with a variety of toppings, ranging from fried eggs and cheese to smoked salmon and sour cream.

3. Papet vaudois: Papet vaudois, a robust and savoury meal that has been a mainstay in local cuisine for generations, will immerse you in the culinary traditions of the Vaud canton. A variety of ingredients, including sausage, pig belly, smoked bacon and white wine, stew together in a thick and savoury sauce in this classic recipe. The recipe is often paired with polenta, a rustic cornmeal dish, to create a filling and cosy supper.

4. fondue fribourgeoise: Beyond the conventional fondue, explore the distinct flavours of fondue fribourgeois, a Fribourg canton speciality. A combination of Vacherin and Gruyère cheeses is used in this variety of the original fondue, resulting in a somewhat sweeter and milder flavour. The inclusion of onions, garlic, and white wine increases the savoury flavour of the fondue.

5. Fillet Mignon with Morilles: Fillet mignon with morilles is a sophisticated meal that turns the basic steak to a gastronomic marvel. Tender fillet mignon medallions art pan-seared to perfection and topped with a rich and creamy sauce made with renowned morille mushrooms, which are noted for their subtle earthy flavour. The meal is often served

with roasted potatoes or veggies, resulting in a sophisticated and enjoyable dining experience.

6. La Truite aux Amandes: Embrace lake flavours with la truite aux amandes, a meal that highlights the region's watery riches. Fresh trout is beautifully poached and served in a creamy almond sauce for a lovely combination of flavours and textures. The delicate sweetness of the almonds balances the delicate flavour of the fish, while the creamy sauce elevates the meal.

7. Chasse: With chasse, a traditional feast that celebrates the abundance of wild game, go on a gastronomic adventure during the Swiss hunting season. This rustic mal combines a variety of game meats cooked to soft perfection in a delicious sauce, including venison, wild boar, and hare. Chasse is often served with spätzle, a kind of egg noodle, or polenta, making for a robust and delicious dinner.

8. lplermagronen: lplermagronen, a classic Alpine meal that has fed shepherds and farmers for centuries, has rustic appeal. This delicious recipe comprises spaghetti tubes cooked in a thick and creamy potato, cheese, and cream sauce. The dish is often topped with crispy fried onions, which add texture and flavour to the creamy foundation.

Montreux provides a diversified culinary landscape that will tantalise your taste buds and deliver an amazing culinary journey, whether you're looking for the comforting warmth of a cheese-based meal or the refined elegance of a gourmet masterpiece.

Gourmet Dining Overlooking Lake Geneva

Montreux, nestled among the magnificent vistas of the Swiss Riviera, provides a dining experience that is both gastronomically and visually appealing. Montreux, with its beautiful views of Lake Geneva and the surrounding Alps, is an ideal setting for indulging in gourmet food. The town's food culture caters to every flavour and choice, from Michelin-starred places to modest lakeside bistros.

1. Le Traiteur: Le Traiteur, a Michelin-starred restaurant known for its inventive food and outstanding service, is the pinnacle of fine dining. Le Traiteur, located inside the Fairmont Le Montreux Palace, provides a gastronomic journey through the seasons, highlighting the best local products and Chef Anton Mosimann's innovative vision. Allow the spectacular views of Lake Geneva and the surrounding Alps to enhance your dining experience, converting it into a memorable

culinary memory as you savour each expertly made dish.

2. La Terrasse: La Terrasse, a lakeside restaurant that perfectly marries superb food with stunning views, exudes charm and elegance. La Terrasse, perched atop the Fairmont Le Montreux Palace, provides a panoramic view of Lake Geneva, the Alps, and the lovely town of Montreux. Chef Francesco Scatamburlo's culinary masterpieces highlight the finest seasonal ingredients, prepared with elegance and presented with flair. Allow the serene setting and stunning vistas to take you to a state of gourmet pleasure while you savour your meal.

3. Le Saveurs: Discover the culinary genius of Le Saveurs, a Michelin-starred restaurant known for its inventive and savoury food. Chef Fabrice Ciocca's culinary innovations highlight the best local ingredients, transforming them into visually gorgeous and gastronomically satisfying meals. Allow the symphony of flavours to dance on your tongue as you indulge in the restaurant's tasting menu, each mouthful a monument to the chef's talent and innovation.

4. Le Restaurant du Parc: Le Restaurant du Parc, a Michelin-starred restaurant hidden inside the Hôtel des Trois Couronnes, transports you to a world of sophisticated luxury. The elegant environment of the restaurant, with luxurious seats and spectacular views of Lake Geneva, gets the setting for an outstanding dining experience. Chef Philippe Chevrier's culinary masterpieces use the freshest seasonal ingredients, meticulously prepared and presented with creativity. Allow the wonderful balance of flavours and the beautiful vistas to create a memorable culinary memory as you savour each dish.

5. La Maison du Poisson: At La Maison du Poisson, a quaint lakeside restaurant famous for its immaculate quality and original flavours, immerse yourself in the world of fresh fish. With its rustic décor and spectacular views of Lake Geneva, the restaurant's warm and friendly environment offers a pleasant backdrop for experiencing the wealth of the sea. The menu offers a diverse assortment of fresh seafood, ranging from juicy grilled fish to delicate seafood platters, all cooked with skill and devotion.

6. La Fourchette: La Fourchette, a lakeside cafe that has become a local favourite, exudes charm and gastronomic pleasures. La Fourchette, located on the Quai de la Rouvenaz, provides a pleasant and friendly ambiance with its cosy décor and stunning views of Lake Geneva. The menu offers a selection of Swiss and French classics made with fresh, seasonal ingredients and a hint of home-style comfort. Allow the calm environment and spectacular vistas to enhance your eating experience while you savour your meal.

7. Le Mirador: At Le Mirador, a lovely restaurant built atop Mont Pèlerin, go on a gastronomic adventure with amazing views. The panoramic terrace of the restaurant offers a breathtaking view of Lake Geneva and the surrounding mountains, giving a magnificent setting for your dining experience. The cuisine includes Swiss and French classics made with fresh, local ingredients with an emphasis on traditional flavours. Allow the stunning sights and serene environment to take you to a state of pure gastronomic ecstasy while you savour your meal.

8. The Old Town of Montreux: Step back in time and enjoy the beauty of Old Montreux at Le Vieux Montreux, a historic Swiss restaurant in the town's core. The rustic décor and pleasant atmosphere of the restaurant's cosy interior create a comfortable backdrop for savouring Swiss culinary classics. The menu includes fondue, raclette, and other classic meals made with fresh, local ingredients and a sense of authenticity. Allow the nostalgic atmosphere and flavours of classic Swiss cuisine to create a memorable dining experience while you enjoy your meal.

Montreux has a diverse culinary landscape that will tantalise your taste buds and provide an unforgettable dining experience, all set against the breathtaking backdrop of Lake Geneva and the surrounding mountains.

Best Cafés for Swiss Chocolate and Pastries

Montreux, set among the stunning surroundings of the Swiss Riviera, is a chocolate and pastry lover's paradise, with a lovely assortment of cosy cafés and classic patisseries where you may indulge in the sweet delights of Swiss culinary traditions.

1. Confiserie Zurcher: Confiserie Zurcher, a famous patisserie that has been a Montreux institution since 1881, welcomes you into a world of chocolate delight. With its wooden countertops, glass displays stocked with scrumptious sweets, and the perfume of freshly made pastries, this lovely restaurant oozes old-world charm. Allow your senses to be fascinated by the rich flavours and beautiful textures as you traverse the tantalising assortment of chocolate masterpieces and artisan pastries. Savour their exquisite pastries, each mouthful a symphony of sweet pleasure, or indulge in their distinctive hot chocolate, a velvety combination of rich cocoa and creamy milk.

2. Chez Gaston: Chez Gaston, a delightful restaurant that has been serving residents and travellers alike since 1929, offers the traditional Swiss café experience. This cosy café, decorated with old posters and soft lighting, provides a

comfortable environment in which to enjoy a choice of Swiss chocolate and pastries. Enjoy the rich flavours of their famous fondue au chocolat, a community dipping experience that includes a pot of melted Swiss chocolate and a variety of fruits, marshmallows, and pastries. Alternatively, savour their flaky croissants, buttery pain au chocolat, and delicate macarons, with each bite demonstrating the patisserie mastery.

3. Pâtisserie de la Gare: Pâtisserie de la Gare, a prominent restaurant near the Montreux train station, will wow you with its sweet fragrances and delightful creations. This lovely bakery has the best Swiss chocolate and pastry workmanship, as well as a broad range of tempting treats to satisfy your sweet taste. Indulge in their decadent chocolate cakes, delicate fruit tartlets, and handmade pralines, each a work of flavour and creativity in its own right. As you savour your sweet delight, let the patisserie colourful environment and kind welcome improve your experience.

4. La Maison du Biscuit: La Maison du Biscuit, a refuge for those seeking a unique and genuine Swiss biscuit experience, welcomes you to a world of biscuit pleasures. This lovely bakery in the heart of Montreux provides a wide variety of homemade

biscuits cooked to perfection using traditional recipes and quality ingredients. Discover the delicate crunch of the meringues and the rich chocolate coating of the orangettes, as well as the subtle sweetness of the sablés. Allow your senses to be charmed by the fragrances and flavours that distinguish Swiss cookie artistry as you explore the delectable assortment of biscuits.

5. Au Fournil: Accept the rustic charm and genuine flavours of Au Fournil, a historic boulangerie-pâtisserie that has served the local community for decades. With its pleasant scent of freshly made bread and pastries, this cosy bakery provides a delectable assortment of Swiss chocolate and pastry goodies. Enjoy their buttery croissants, flaky pain au chocolat, and rich chocolate cakes, each mouthful a monument to the bakery's dedication to traditional processes and high-quality ingredients. Allow the warm ambiance and nostalgic charm of the bakery to take you to a world of classic Swiss baking while you savour your sweet treat.

Montreux has a broad selection of cafés and enterprises where you may indulge in the sweet delights of Swiss chocolate and pastries, whether you're looking for the polished elegance of a famous patisserie or the rustic charm of a typical bakery. Each taste will be a symphony of sweet joy, generating lasting memories of your culinary travels in Montreux, from the rich flavours of classic fondue au chocolat to the delicate artistry of artisan cookies and pastries.

POPULAR MUSEUMS

Montreux Jazz Heritage

Montreux, nestle among the magnificent landscapes of the Swiss Riviera, is not only known for its mesmerising beauty and cultural attractions, but it also has a thriving museum culture that caters to a wide variety of interests and preferences. Montreux provides an amazing experience for anyone looking to immerse themselves in the town's cultural tapestry, with museums delving into the town's rich musical tradition as well as institutions presenting art and history.

1. Queen Studio Experience: The Queen Studio Experience transports you to the renowned world of Queen and the creative energy of Freddie Mercury. This one-of-a-kind museum, built in the old studio where Queen produced their legendary album "Made in Japan, " offers an intimate look into the band's creative process and their lasting effect on music history. As you tour the studio, you'll come upon a treasure mine of artefacts, such as handwritten lyrics, vintage instruments, and theatrical costumes that have been maintained in their original state. Immerse yourself in the music with interactive displays, listen to restored

recordings in the control room, and let Queen's energy carry you back to a period of innovative music and iconic performances.

2. Musée du Vieux Montreux: Visit the Musée du Vieux Montreux, a delightful museum located in a 16th-century vineyard house, to immerse yourself in Montreux's history. This fascinating museum takes visitors on a trip through time, highlighting the town's rich history and traditions. Explore a collection of permanent displays that trace Montreux's evolution from a tiny fishing hamlet to a cosmopolitan tourist destination. Explore artefacts, documents, and images that depict the town's social, economic, and cultural development. Allow the tales of the past to come life as you browse the museum's displays, gaining a better understanding for Montreux's distinct personality and timeless charm.

3. Montreux Museum: Immerse yourself in the worlds of art and history at the Montreux Museum, a large institution with a wide collection. The museum, housed in a former lakeside mansion, presents an enthralling mix of permanent and temporary exhibits. Discover a plethora of archaeological artefacts, paintings, and sculptures spanning millennia of creativity. Explore the

region's history, from ancient times to the present day cultural scene. Discover the story behind the masterpieces of notable painters such as Ferdinand Hodler and Alexandre Blanchet. Allow the creative expressions and historical tales to grab your imagination and expand your awareness of Montreux's cultural history as you tour the museum's galleries.

4. Claude Nobs Foundation: The Claude Nobs Foundation honours the visionary originator of the Montreux Jazz Festival, Claude Nobs. This non-profit organisation, situated in Nobs' old home, pays honour to his life and love for music. Discover a selection of exhibits showcasing Nobs' personal collection of musical instruments, memorabilia, and pictures. Explore the history of the Montreux Jazz Festival, learning about its growth and effect on the world of music. Allow the spirit of Nobs and his continuing enthusiasm for music to inspire you as you immerse yourself in the displays, leaving you with a new understanding for the tremendous effect of music in our lives.

5. Musee du Jeu et de l'Imaginaire (MUJI): The Musee du Jeu et de l'Imaginaire (MUJI) will spark your imagination and teach you about the power of play. This one-of-a-kind museum devoted to the

world of toys and games provides an interactive and fascinating experience for visitors of all ages. Discover a diverse range of toys from throughout the globe, ranging from classic wooden toys to modern technological devices. Explore the history of toys and their significance in child development, as well as interactive exhibitions that foster creativity and imagination. Allow your inner kid to come alive as you wander the museumcreative rooms and rediscover the pleasure of play in all its inventive forms.

The museums of Montreux provide a broad and engaging tour through the town's musical legacy, creative manifestations, and historical tales. Each museum offers an exceptional experience that will improve your awareness of Montreux's distinctive personality and its ongoing cultural importance, from the renowned world of Queen to the enthralling tales of the past.

Chillon Castle

Chillon Castle, perched on a rocky island in the middle of Lake Geneva's magnificent surroundings, stands as an everlasting tribute to history, a compelling landmark that has seen centuries of alteration and strife. Chillon Castle has played an important part in the region's history, from its modest origins as a Roman outpost to its function as a formidable fortification and royal house, leaving behind a rich tapestry of myths and legends.

A Power and Defence Stronghold

Chillon Castle dates back to the 11th century, when it was established as a strategic fortification controlling the Alpine passes and trade routes around Lake Geneva. Its enormous fortress-like construction, with high walls and strategically placed towers, acted as a powerful defense against invaders, shielding the area from the turmoil of mediaeval warfare.

A Royal Residence

Chillon Castle moved into the hands of the Counts of Savoy in the 13th century, a strong family that dominated over the area for generations. The castle experienced substantial alterations throughout their reign, developing from a military fortress to an elegant royal home. The Counts of Savoy added great halls, luxurious rooms, and elaborate defences to the castle, making it into a symbol of their power and dignity.

An Intriguing and Captivating Location

Despite its magnificence, Chillon Castle saw some of history's worst moments. Its subterranean dungeons, with their darkly lighted rooms and dismal ambiance, housed people considered adversaries of the Counts of Savoy. François Bonivard, a Genevan patriot who spent six years imprisoned inside the castle's walls, etched his name and the date of his incarceration on a pillar that still survives as a sad reminder of the castle's history.

A Literary Insight

Literary titans have taken note of Chillon Castle's enchanting charm. Lord Byron wrote his renowned poem "The Prisoner of Chillon, " inspired by the castle's scenic backdrop and tales of incarceration, immortalising the castle's fame and presenting its stories to a broader audience.

A Historical Treasure Trove

Chillon Castle survives now as a fascinating historical remnant, a stunning landmark that has been methodically repaired and protected. Through exhibitions and interactive displays, visitors may explore the castle's labyrinthine halls, marvel at its architectural wonders, and dig into the castle's rich history. Chillon Castle provides a trip through time, affording a look into the region's stormy history and the ongoing impact of this historic structure.

Swiss Museum of Games

The Swiss Museum of Games, or Musée Suisse du Jeu, is a unique and intriguing institution that celebrates the world of games in all its many manifestations, nestled among the magnificent surroundings of the Swiss Riviera. From ancient gaming artefacts to modern digital innovations, the museum takes visitors on a journey through time and culture, demonstrating the everlasting power of play and its relevance in human history.

A Treasure Chest of Delightful Delights

The Swiss Museum of Games holds a significant collection of over 10,000 games from all over the world, spanning centuries. Visitors may explore the museum's exhibits in an interactive and engaging way, uncovering a treasure trove of amusing pleasures that have captivated generations. The museum's collection displays the unlimited imagination and ingenuity that have formed the world of games, from classic board games and card games to modern digital innovations.

A Cultural and Time Travel Journey

The displays in the museum dig into the rich history of games, tracing their progression from ancient roots to present popularity. Visitors may examine the evolution of games throughout numerous cultures and civilizations by discovering the first gaming artefacts, such as dice and board games uncovered at archaeological sites. The museum's collection demonstrates how games have been used as means for amusement, education, and cultural expression throughout history.

A Celebration of Imagination and Play

The Swiss Museum of Games is founded on a deep respect for the power of play and its potential to spark imagination, develop creativity, and bring people together. The interactive displays at the museum encourage visitors to participate with the games on show, immersing themselves in the fun sensations that have enthralled generations. The museum invites visitors to rediscover the pleasure of play and its transforming impact, whether it's rolling the dice in a classic board game or navigating the hurdles of a digital puzzle.

A Learning and Discovery Hub

The Swiss Museum of Games, in addition to its intriguing exhibitions, also functions as a centre for learning and exploration, providing a plethora of educational tools and programmes. Children may participate in interactive workshops and activities that promote cognitive development and creativity. Adults may learn about gaming history via lectures, seminars, and research possibilities. The museum's educational mission guarantees that the history of play and its relevance in human civilization inspire and enhance future generations.

Charlie Chaplin's World in Vevey

Charlie Chaplin's World in Vevey, nestled among the magnificent surroundings of the Swiss Riviera, offers you to enter the wonderful domain of one of cinema's most renowned personalities. This engaging museum, based in Chaplin's old Swiss mansion, provides an immersive and unique trip into the iconic filmmaker's life and work.

A Look at Chaplin's Life

You'll be taken into the world of Charlie Chaplin, the man behind the renowned moustache and bowler hat, as you begin on your Chaplin's World trip. Discover Chaplin's private life, hobbies, and the creative process behind his renowned films at the Manoir, his former home.

A Film Festival of Cinematic Brilliance

Enter the Hollywood Studio to be transported to the sets of Chaplin's most renowned flicks. Explore recreated settings, get immersed in the magic of filmmaking, and discover the eternal attraction of Chaplin's cinematic masterpieces.

Chaplin's Imagination Playground

Enter Chaplin's Park, a charming outdoor place inspired by Charlie Chaplin's lively personality. Explore the fun world of Charlie Chaplin by engaging in interactive displays, discovering hidden surprises, and letting your imagination fly.

A Laughter and Inspirational World

Allow Chaplin's humour, ingenuity, and lasting legacy to inspire you throughout your Chaplin's World experience. Discover the man behind the legend, the artist who won millions of hearts with his timeless films and fascinating characters.

A Must-See for Chaplin and Film Lovers

Charlie Chaplin's World in Vevey offers a fascinating trip into the life and work of a cinematic legend, whether you're a lifetime Chaplin fan or just looking for a compelling cultural experience. Allow Chaplin's World to pique your interest, take you to the golden era of Hollywood, and leave you with a renewed respect for cinema's lasting impact.

DAY TRIPS

Excursion to Zermatt and the Matterhorn

Explore Zermatt, a charming hamlet set within the gorgeous Swiss Alps, and marvel at the renowned Matterhorn, a peak that has fascinated climbers and explorers for centuries.

Zermatt Journey

Begin your journey with a picturesque train trip to Zermatt, a car-free hamlet known for its peace and magnificent mountain vistas. Allow the breathtaking panoramas of snow-capped peaks and green landscapes to fill you with anticipation as you rise through the valleys and thread your way into the Alps.

Entry into Zermatt

Step into a world of alpine beauty in Zermatt, where charming chalets and classic Swiss architecture combine harmoniously with the spectacular mountain background. Stroll around the village's cobblestone streets, which are dotted with quaint stores, cosy cafés, and welcoming restaurants, and absorb in the peaceful ambiance and friendly friendliness of the residents.

Climb to Gornergrat

Gornergrat, a mountain cogwheel train that takes you to a height of 3, 089 metres, is a must-see. As you rise, take in the beautiful view of the surrounding peaks, especially the legendary Matterhorn, which looms majestically in front of you.

Matterhorn Exploration

From Gornergrat, take a hiking route or a cable car to reach even higher viewing spots with unrivalled views of the Matterhorn's towering peak. Capture the mountain's beauty in all of its moods, from snow-kissed splendour into brilliant colours in summer.

Delicious Culinary Delights in Zermatt

Zermatt's gastronomic pleasures combine traditional Swiss cuisine with foreign flavours. At one of the village's numerous cafés and restaurants, savour the rich flavours of raclette, fondue, and meat meat dishes, or choose for lighter food.

Swiss Spa Rejuvenation

After a day of touring, relax in one of Zermatt's numerous spas, which provide a wide range of health services. Immerse yourself in the therapeutic waters of thermal baths, treat yourself to revitalising massages, and let the calm surroundings to soothe your body and spirit.

A Delightful Departure

As your trip comes to an end, say goodbye to Zermatt, taking with you memories of the beautiful Matterhorn, the lovely hamlet, and the wonderful hospitality of the Swiss Alps. Leave with a deeper appreciation for this mountain paradise's beauty and tranquillity.

Geneva

Geneva, the embodiment of a cosmopolitan city, combines its rich history, cultural legacy, and international flare in a seamless manner. Geneva provides a day trip full of engaging activities, from visiting its historic buildings to immersing yourself in its thriving arts scene.

Morning:

1. Take a stroll around Lake Geneva: Begin your day with a walk along the beaches of Lake Geneva, the city's glistening focal point. Enjoy the tranquilly of the waterfront promenade while taking in the stunning views of the lake and neighbouring mountains.

2. Pay a visit to the Jet d'Eau: Witness the magnificent Jet d'Eau fountain, Geneva's landmark, as it launches a jet of water 140 metres into the air. Capture the mesmerising beauty of the fountain against the background of Lake Geneva and the metropolis.

3. Visit the Old Town: Explore Geneva's picturesque Old Town, a maze of cobblestone lanes, ancient structures, and tiny stores. Wander around the bustling Place du Bourg-de-Four and see the 12th-century St. Peter's Cathedral, a stunning Gothic masterpiece.

Afternoon:

1. Explore History at the Palais des Nations: At the Palais des Nations, the headquarters of the United Nations and other international organisations,

immerse yourself in the realm of international diplomacy. Explore the stunning architecture, interactive exhibitions, and learn about the UN's worldwide operations.

2. Visit the Reformation Museum: The Reformation Museum, situated in the historic Maison Tavel, transports visitors to the heart of the Protestant Reformation. Explore exhibitions in Geneva that document the history of the Reformation, highlighting its influence on religion, culture, and politics.

3. Take a look at the Floral Clock: Admire the exquisite Floral Clock, a one-of-a-kind watch covered with over 12, 000 flowers. The clock's design morphs into a stunning tapestry of colourful blossoms as the seasons change.

Evening:

1. Enjoy Swiss Cuisine: Treat your taste buds to Geneva's gastronomic treasures. At one of the city's fashionable restaurants, savour classic Swiss dishes like raclette, fondue, and rösti, or choose for contemporary fusion food.

2. Take in the Arts Scene: Immerse yourself in the dynamic artistic scene of Geneva. Explore modern art galleries or attend a classical music concert in one of the city's historic venues after seeing a thrilling production at the Grand Théâtre de Genève.

3. Take a Lake Geneva Night Cruise: Finish your day with an unforgettable night sail on Lake Geneva. Glide over the calm waters, taking in the city's lit skyline and the dazzling lights that reflect on the lake's surface.

Carry with you the memories of a city that perfectly integrates its rich history with its global energy, leaving you with a great appreciation for its distinctive charm and lasting appeal as you travel from Geneva.

Lavaux Vineyards

The Lavaux Vineyards, a UNESCO World Heritage Site famed for its spectacular beauty, rich history, and superb wines, are hidden among the gorgeous landscapes of the Swiss Riviera, along the beaches of Lake Geneva. Lavaux welcomes you to go on an exciting wine-tasting trip with its terraced vines pouring down the slopes and affording spectacular views of the lake and neighbouring mountains.

A Trip Through Time and Terroir

Allow the magnificent backdrop of Lavaux to take you through time as you begin your wine-tasting tour. Consider the Benedictine monks who planted these vineyards in the 11th century, changing the landscape with their cunning and commitment. Discover Lavaux's distinct terroir, where the interaction of soil, climate, and grape varietals creates wines of extraordinary character and elegance.

A Flavour Symphony

Experience the symphony of flavours at one of Lavaux's numerous vineyards. Chasselas, the region's trademark grape, is recognised for its sharp acidity and invigorating minerality. Enjoy the rich, nuanced flavours of Pinot Noir, which is well suited to Lavaux's cold environment and sunny slopes. Discover the region's lesser-known beauties, such as the fragrant Chasselas Musqué and the subtle Gamaret, each delivering a distinct reflection of Lavaux's terroir.

A Delectable Delight

Lavaux's gastronomic pleasures will round out your wine-tasting experience. Local cheeses, such as the creamy Vacherin and the peppery Tomme Vaudoise, go well with the region's wines. Savour the beautiful combination of flavours in classic Swiss meals like raclette or fondue.

A Scenic Adventure

Immerse yourself in the spectacular beauty of the terrain by enjoying a picturesque walk or bike ride through the Lavaux Vineyards. Admire the spectacular views of Lake Geneva and the neighbouring Alps as you climb the terraced slopes. Discover secret towns, quaint cafés, and welcoming vineyards, all of which contribute to the region's distinct appeal.

A Tapestry of Culture

Explore Lavaux's unique cultural tapestry, where traditions have been handed down through centuries. Visit local artists who demonstrate their skills in winemaking, cheesemaking, and carpentry. Immerse yourself in the vivid essence of the area by attending a traditional wine festival or folk music event.

A Long-Term Impression

Allow the memories of this wonderful location to linger as your Lavaux wine-tasting journey comes to an end. Carry the symphony of flavours, the stunning environment, and the kindness of the people with you as a monument to Lavaux's winemaking tradition's continuing heritage.

Rochers-de-Naye

Rochers-de-Naye, nestled among the stunning landscapes of the Swiss Alps, provides an amazing spectacular mountain journey, offering panoramic panoramas, exhilarating activities, and a calm retreat into nature's embrace.

Ascending to the Peak

Your Rochers-de-Nay excursion starts with a picturesque ride aboard the Montreux-Glion Railway, a vintage cogwheel train. As you climb the mountain, take in the changing scenery, from the lush lowlands to the snow-capped peaks that gradually appear.

A View From Every Angle

Allow yourself to be charmed by the spectacular landscape that unfolds before you as you reach the peak of Rochers-de-Naye at a height of 2, 042 metres. Admire the dazzling length of Lake Geneva, situated among the beautiful Alps. Take in the panoramic views of the neighbouring mountains, which are painted in tones of green, brown, and white.

A Destination for Outdoor Enthusiasts

Rochers-de-Nay is a paradise for outdoor lovers, featuring activities for people of all ages and interests. Hike along well-maintained routes to uncover secret vistas and alpine meadows filled with wildflowers. Take a relaxing dip at the alpine lake, surrounded by nature's calm splendour.

Culinary Delights Surrounded by Breathtaking Views

Enjoy the gastronomic pleasures of Rochers-de-Naye, where traditional Swiss cuisine meets the spectacular Alpine setting. Choose from a selection of restaurants, each with a distinct eating experience and breathtaking views. Indulge in rich delicacies like raclette or fondue, or go lighter with a hint of regional flavour.

A Relaxing Getaway

Get away from the rush and bustle of daily life and relax in the ambiance of Rochers-de-Naye. Relax on the patio in the sun, letting the calm mountain air caress your face. Find a peaceful area among the alpine meadows, surrounded by nature's noises, and just breathe in the peace of the moment.

A Cherished Memory

As your trip to Rochers-de-Naye comes to an end, enjoy the memories you've made. Take with you the stunning views, exhilarating outdoor adventures, and peaceful moments of solitude. Depart Rochers-de-Nay with a fresh appreciation for the majesty and grandeur of the Swiss Alps, which will be imprinted on your heart forever.

PRACTICAL TIPS FOR THRILL-SEEKERS

Emergency Contacts and Medical Facilities

Emergency Contacts

Police: 117
Ambulance: 144
Fire Department: 118
Emergency Medical Service (EMS): 144

Medical Facilities

1. Hôpital Riviera-Chablais: Avenue de Belmont 40, 1820 Montreux, Switzerland.

2. Clinique Suisse Montreux: GrandRue 3, 1820 Montreux, Switzerland.

3. Centre Médical du Lac: Rue des Anciens-Moulins 10, 1820 Montreux, Switzerland.

4. Cabinet médical de la Gare: Rue du Grammont 2, 1820 Montreux, Switzerland.

5. Pédiatrie de Montreux: Rue de la Gare 2, 1820 Montreux, Switzerland.

Pharmacies

1. Pharmacie de la Gare: Rue de la Gare 39, 1820 Montreux, Switzerland.

2. Pharmacie du Centre: Grand'Rue 36, 1820 Montreux, Switzerland.

3. Pharmacie du Casino: Avenue du Casino 28, 1820 Montreux, Switzerland.

4. Pharmacie du Lac: Avenue du Lac 1, 1820 Montreux, Switzerland.

5. Pharmacie du Rivage: Rue du Rivage 3, 1820 Montreux, Switzerland.

Dental Clinics

1. Dentiste Montreux: Rue du Grammont 2, 1820 Montreux, Switzerland.

2. Centre Dentaire du Lac: Rue du Lac 1, 1820 Montreux, Switzerland.

3. Clinique Dentaire Montreux: Avenue du Casino 28, 1820 Montreux, Switzerland.

4. Cabinet Dentaire Dr. Jean-Pierre Bieri: Avenue du Casino 28, 1820 Montreux, Switzerland.

5. Cabinet Dentaire Dr. Michel Jeannerat: Avenue du Casino 28, 1820 Montreux, Switzerland.

Veterinary Clinics

1. Cabinet Vétérinaire Gambetta: Rue Gambetta 1, 1820 Montreux, Switzerland.

2. Clinique Vétérinaire du Lac: Avenue du Lac 1, 1820 Montreux, Switzerland.

3. Clinique Vétérinaire de la Riviera: Avenue de Belmont 40, 1820 Montreux, Switzerland.

4. Centre Vétérinaire du Léman: Rue de la Gare 2, 1820 Montreux, Switzerland.

5. Clinique Vétérinaire des Anciens Moulins: Rue des Anciens-Moulins 10, 1820 Montreux, Switzerland.

Transportation Options in Montreux

Montreux has a range of transit alternatives to meet your requirements and interests, whether you're visiting the town, exploring the surrounding countryside, or just travelling between locations. Here's a rundown of the main Montreux transit options:

Trains: Montreux is well-connected to the Swiss railway network, giving it a perfect starting point for train excursions around the area. The Montreux-Oberland Bernois Railway (MOB) runs along Lake Geneva's coasts, linking Montreux to Vevey, Château-de-Chillon, and Les Pléiades. The Swiss Federal Railways (SBB) offers direct services to major cities such as Geneva, Lausanne, and Bern, as well as links to the rest of Switzerland and Europe.

Buses: Montreux has a well-developed bus system that services the town and its neighbouring regions. Transports Montreux-Vevey-Riviera (MVR) maintains a bus network linking Montreux to other cities, villages, and attractions like as Glion, Rochers-de-Naye, and the Lavaux vineyards.

Boats: Lake Geneva is an important part of Montreux's transportation network. The Compagnie Générale de Navigation (CGN) runs frequent boat services across Lake Geneva, linking Montreux to other lakefront cities like as Vevey, Lausanne, and Nyon. These gorgeous boat cruises allow access to major landmarks such as Chillon Castle and the Lavaux vineyards, as well as a unique view of the region's surroundings.

Taxi and Limousine Services: Taxis are easily accessible in Montreux and may be summoned from the street or hired over the phone. There are also many automobile rental firms in town, giving handy choices for people who prefer to explore the area at their own leisure.

Funiculars and cable cars: Montreux has a lovely funicular train, the Territet-Glion funicular, which links Territet, a lakeside resort, to Glion, an elevation settlement. This picturesque journey provides stunning views of Lake Geneva and the neighbouring Alps. Furthermore, cable cars allow access to the Rochers-de-Naye top, which offers panoramic views of the area.

Cycling and walking: Montreux is a walking-friendly town with well-kept pavements and walkways. Walking around the town centre, the lakeside promenade, and the lovely neighbourhoods is a terrific way to see everything. Cycling is another popular activity, with designated bike tracks along the lakeside and across the surrounding countryside.

Tickets for Public Transportation: In Montreux, many public transport tickets are available to meet a variety of travel demands and durations. The Montreux Riviera Card providers unrestricted travel throughout the area on trains, buses, and boats, as well as discounts on attractions and activities. Single-day tickets and multi-day passes for certain zones or modes of travel are also available.

Accessibility: Montreux is dedicated to making public transit accessible to everybody. Many bus stops and rail stations have ramps and lifts, and most public transit vehicles are wheelchair accessible. Accessibility information is easily accessible from local transit operators.

Safety Precautions for Outdoor Adventures

Outdoor experiences may be thrilling and gratifying, but it's essential to prioritise safety and take proper steps to reduce hazards and guarantee a happy end. Here are some important safety precautions for outdoor activities:

1. Thoroughly plan and prepare:

- Select the Right Activity: Choose an activity that corresponds to your skill level, physical fitness, and experience. Don't overestimate your ability or do tasks that are beyond your abilities.

- Research and Information Gathering: Learn about the location you want to visit, including weather conditions, geography, possible risks, and emergency protocols.

- Review Weather Updates: Monitor weather predictions on a regular basis and be prepared for unexpected changes or unfavourable circumstances.

2. Dress Properly:

- Wear Appropriate Clothing: Dress in clothes appropriate for the forecasted weather and activity level. Think about moisture-wicking clothes, sunscreen, and proper footwear.

- Carry the Necessities: Pack a first-aid kit, navigation equipment, a map, several layers of clothes, a waterproof shell, a headlamp or torch, and enough of drink and food in a backpack.

3. Explain Your Plans:

- Notify Others: Inform someone of your plan, including your estimated return time, the site you'll be visiting, and emergency contact information.

- Use Communication Devices: Always have a fully charged mobile phone or other communication device on hand in case of an emergency or unexpected event.

4. Develop Safety Habits:

- Remain Vigilant and Aware: Be aware of your surroundings, keep an eye out for any threats, and avoid distractions.

- Respect Trail Markers and Signs: Respect trail markers and signs, and never wander off-trail without sufficient direction and preparedness.

- Leave No Trace Policy: Reduce your environmental effect by practising good outdoor manners. Pack out all rubbish, leave natural places alone, and be mindful of animals.

5. Know Your Limits and Be Flexible:

- Be Prepared: Begin softly and progressively pick up the speed as your body warms up. Take pauses as required and don't push yourself above your capabilities.

- Be Flexible: Be ready to change your plans into changing weather conditions, unanticipated hurdles, or unexpected occurrences.

- Know When to Turn Back: Don't be afraid to turn back if situations get too difficult or dangerous. It's always better to be safe than sorry.

6. Ask for Help When Necessary:

- Do Not Be Afraid to Ask for Help: If you run into problems or need assistance, don't be afraid to ask for help from other explorers, park rangers, or emergency officials.

- Be Aware of Local Emergency Procedures: Be aware of local emergency procedures, including how to call emergency services and activate emergency beacons if necessary.

Remember that safety should always come first while going on outdoor excursions. You may minimise hazards and maximise pleasure of your outdoor excursions by planning properly, preparing sufficiently, and practising responsible behaviours.

CONCLUSION

As the final chapter of the Montreux Travel Guide 2024 unfolds, we invite you to reflect on the tapestry of experiences woven throughout your journey in this Alpine wonderland. From the shores of Lake Geneva to the dizzying heights of the Swiss Alps, Montreux has opened its arms to you, offering a symphony of culture, culinary delights, and hidden gems.

As your guide, we aimed to transport you beyond the confines of the ordinary and into a realm where every cobblestone street, every panoramic vista, and every gastronomic delight becomes a cherished memory. Our words have been the brushstrokes painting the canvas of your imagination, allowing you to visualize the breathtaking landscapes, taste the exquisite flavours, and feel the pulse of this vibrant city.

In Montreux, the absence of maps was not a limitation but an opportunity – an invitation to wander, to get lost, and to stumble upon the unexpected. It's a testament to the belief that the true essence of a place cannot be confined to geographical coordinates; rather, it is etched in the stories, shared laughter, and chance encounters with locals that colour your memories.

As you close the pages of this guide, may the spirit of Montreux linger in your heart. Whether you sought the thrill of outdoor adventures, revealed in the cultural tapestry, or simply savoured the tranquillity of the lakeside, we hope this journey has left an indelible mark on your travel repertoire.

Montreux, with its timeless allure, has been more than a destination; it has been an experience – a celebration of the extraordinary in the ordinary, a reminder that the joy of travel lies not just in reaching a destination but in the stories you collect along the way.

Our wish for you is that the memories forged in Montreux become a source of inspiration for future explorations, igniting the spark of wanderlust within you. As the final chapter concludes, the story of Montreux continues in your heart, ready to be retold in the tales you share with fellow adventurers.

Thank you for allowing us to be a part of your Montreux journey. Until the next adventure, may your travels be filled with wonder, discovery, and the enduring magic that only exploration can unveil.

Safe travels, and may the spirit of Montreux accompany you wherever your next adventure takes you.

Made in the USA
Las Vegas, NV
26 April 2025